ZFS ON LINUX:

INTERNALS AND ADMINISTRATION

WILLIAM SPEIRS PHD

ACKNOWLEDGEMENT

This book would not have come together, and certainly not at the speed at which it did, without the help of two people: Tom Caputi and Heidi Smith. Tom designed and implemented native encryption for ZFS. After a bit of prodding, he authored the chapter on Native ZFS Encryption and the section on the same topic in Chapter 8.

Heidi is responsible for taking my raw text and turning it into a work of art. She created all the diagrams you see in this book, the layout of the book, and the cover art. Without her artistic abilities, this book would be little more than words in a text file.

Finally, I would like to acknowledge both Austin McChord, Founder and CEO of Datto, and Robert Gibbons, CTO of Datto. They both provided me the opportunity to take time from my regular work to author this book.

Table of Contents

1. **INTRODUCTION** — 7
    a. ZFS at Datto — 8
    b. Tradeoff of ZFS — 9

2. **VIRTUAL DEVICES** — 13
    a. Mirroring — 15
    b. RAID-Z — 16
    c. Performance — 18
    d. SLOG and L2ARC — 19

3. **ZFS POOLS** — 23
    a. Stripes — 24
    b. ZFS Object Tree — 25
    c. Dnodes — 27
    d. Consistency — 29
    e. ZFS Attribute Processor — 29
    f. ZFS POSIX Layer — 30
    g. Snapshots and Clones — 30

4. **ZFS FILE SYSTEM** — 33
    a. Checkpoints — 34
    b. ZFS Intent Log — 35
    c. Writing Data — 36
    d. ARC and L2ARC Cache — 37
    e. ZFS Properties — 41

5. **NATIVE ZFS ENCRYPTION** — 47
    a. A Brief Overview of Encryption — 48
    b. Advantages of Native ZFS Encryption — 50
    c. Implementation — 51

6. WORKING WITH VDEVS — 53
   a. `zpool` Command Basics — 54
   b. Mirrored VDEVs — 55
   c. RAID-Z — 61
   d. SLOG and L2ARC VDEVs — 62

7. WORKING WITH DATASETS — 65
   a. ZFS Commands — 67
   b. Managing File Systems — 68
   c. Managing Snapshots — 71
   d. Managing Clones — 74
   e. Managing ZFS Volumes — 75
   f. Quotas and Reservations — 77

8. ADVANCED FILESYSTEM FEATURES — 79
   a. Compression — 80
   b. Deduplication — 82
   c. Encryption — 83
   d. Scrub and Resilver — 87
   e. ZFS Send and Receive — 88
   f. Bookmarks — 92

9. PERFORMANCE AND TUNING — 95
   a. Collecting Stats — 96
   b. Prefetching — 99
   c. Transaction Group Tuning — 101
   d. Scrubs and Resilvers — 102
   e. `volblocksize` and `recordsize` — 103
   f. Databases — 105

CHAPTER 1

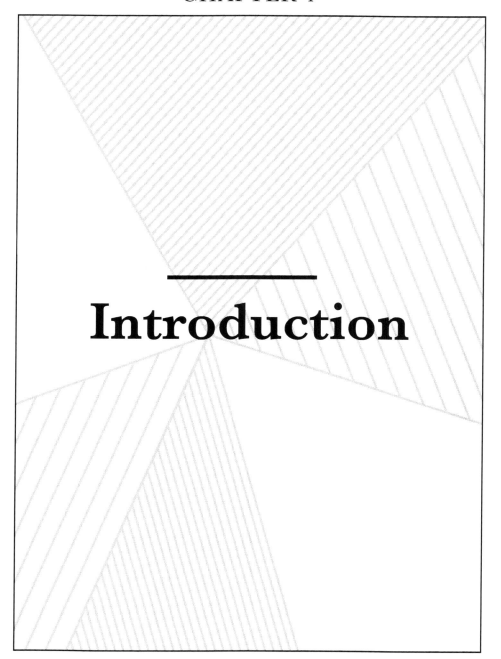

Introduction

INTRO

A handful of books have been written about the open source Zettabyte Filesystem (ZFS) including "FreeBSD Mastery: ZFS" and "FreeBSD Mastery Advanced ZFS" both by Jude and Lucas. So, why write another book on ZFS? Because this book focuses on running ZFS on Linux, not BSD or Illumos. All examples in this book use an Ubuntu server, and the performance tuning options are Linux specific. There is obvious overlap between ZFS on BSD and ZFS on Linux, but enough differences exist that it merited writing a Linux specific book about ZFS. This book also dispels a few myths about ZFS that were never true, or are no longer true with the most current version of ZFS. This book also includes, for the first time, documentation on native encryption for ZFS.

ZFS AT DATTO

Given that I work for Datto, Inc., I have a unique opportunity to see one of the largest, if not the largest, deployments of ZFS on Linux in the world. Datto is a Backup and Disaster Recovery company that stores more than (as of the time this book was published) 250 petabytes (PB) of data in ZFS. We have seen ZFS work, and more importantly fail in spectacular ways. Datto has also advanced ZFS by adding native encryption (see Chapter 5, Native ZFS Encryption).

Datto's success and stability is enabled by ZFS's unique ability to replicate datasets between devices (see Chapter 8, Advanced Filesystem Features). Because Datto was able to build a successful company based on the work of OpenZFS, we wanted to write a book as a way to give back to the open source community.

TRADEOFFS OF ZFS

ZFS is not a one-size-fits-all filesystem. There are some cases where ZFS simply does not perform as well as other filesystems. However, in most cases, the benefits from ZFS far outweigh any costs imposed by its design. To make an informed decision about whether ZFS is the right choice for your application, you must understand the tradeoffs made while designing ZFS.

The biggest difference between ZFS and a traditional filesystem, like ext2/3/4, is that ZFS is a non-overwriting, or copy-on-write filesystem. This means that a block in the middle of a file is never overwritten when modified in ZFS. Instead, a new copy of the block is created and written elsewhere in the filesystem. The advantage is that writes in ZFS are sequential across all modifications to all files in a given time period. A traditional filesystem, writes are scattered across the filesystem as the blocks associated with the various files are updated. When data is read, the opposite is true. In most traditional filesystems reads are sequential. However, in ZFS reads are scattered across the disk. ZFS is able to remain performant because of the Adaptive Replacement Cache (ARC) (see Chapter 4, Filesystem).

While the ARC helps to make ZFS efficient during reads, it also uses up more memory in the system than necessary. Linux already heavily caches disk I/O. Unfortunately, there is no way to disable this cache in Linux, so administrators have two options: double-cache disk I/O or disable the ZFS ARC. In traditional filesystems written specifically for Linux, the caching is left to the Linux kernel and focus is solely on providing filesystem functionality.

INTRO

Because ZFS is a copy-on-write filesystem, it requires more space to operate than a traditional filesystem. In ext2/3/4 for example, if the filesystem has only 50MB of free space remaining, the filesystem happily allows an update to the middle 100 MB of a 1GB file. In ZFS however, you are unlikely to be able to perform this action. This is because ZFS requires 100MB of extra space to write this new data. The same is true for deleting data. In ZFS, deleting data requires space. So keep disks at a maximum of 80% filled for ZFS to operate without issue.

ZFS, being both a filesystem and a volume manager, has advantages over using something like LVM and ext2/3/4 on Linux. One such example is the write-hole problem found with traditional RAID configurations. A write-hole occurs when data is written to the many disks in the RAID, but a failure occurs. It is unknown to which disks data has been persisted, and to which disks it has not. Therefore, repairs can potentially create garbage data. ZFS does not suffer from this problem because all writes are atomic. If a failure occurs before a write is completed, the write is not accepted and the filesystem is rolled back to its previous state during recovery.

ZFS also offers snapshots and clones of filesystems, because of the tight integration of the volume manager and the filesystem. Traditional Linux setups require the volume manager to take care of snapshots and clones, with little regard to the filesystem that is using the volumes.

Traditional filesystems write blocks of a fixed size. If this size is not compatible with the application writing the data, then inefficiencies can occur. For example, if the block size of a filesystem is 512 bytes, but the record size of a database is 4,096 bytes, four block pointers are updated with each written record. ZFS, on the other hand, has configurable (within limits) block sizes that can perfectly match the record size of the database. This limits the amount of metadata overhead required.

Testing is simply the best way to know if ZFS works for a specific use case. Leverage the performance tuning found in Chapter 9, Performance Tuning, to help make ZFS as performant as possible. Keep in mind that raw read and write speed is only one dimension of performance. Reliability in the face of failure, ease of administration, and security are also factors to keep in mind when making decisions. If your use case is anything like Datto's, we highly recommend ZFS!

CHAPTER 2

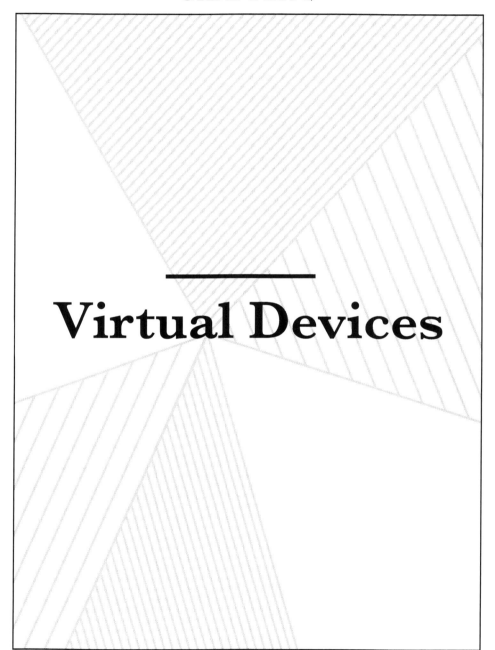

Virtual Devices

VIRTUAL DEVICES

As mentioned in the introduction, ZFS serves as both a volume manager and a filesystem. This chapter on virtual devices (vdevs), along with Chapter 3, ZFS Pools, focuses on the volume management portion of ZFS.

Virtual devices are divided into two categories: physical and logical. A physical vdev is typically a block device in Linux. A physical vdev can be backed by several different types of physical storage: hard disk, a partition on a disk, a network block device, a set of disks in a RAID configuration, or even a file in another filesystem. Just about anything that can read and write bytes is a physical vdev.

Each physical vdev contains a vdev label. The label contains, among other things, an array of uberblocks, and a name/value list. We will see the importance of uberblocks in Chapter 3, ZFS Pools, but for now simply take note that uberblocks are stored in the vdev label of the physical vdevs. The label also contains information about the physical vdev's parent, and all of the parent's children. For example, in Figure 1, the labels for vdev B also contains information for vdev C and their parent "mirror."

The information contained in vdev labels is extremely important to the correct operation of ZFS. Because of the significance of these labels, ZFS maintains four copies of the label: two at the front and two at the back. While ZFS typically uses copy-on-write semantics for all data in the system, vdev labels are placed when the vdev is added to a pool, and never moved. Instead, the labels are overwritten two at a time. The first labels at the front and back of the vdev are updated first. If the system crashes during this write, then the second labels at the front and back are still usable. After the first labels in each position are updated, the second labels are updated. Given the four copies and the label, it is nearly impossible to find a corrupted vdev label.

Logical vdevs are the composition of physical vdevs. Vdevs are composed in a tree structure of up to 232 virtual devices. The leaf nodes of this tree structure are the physical vdevs, and the interior nodes are the logical vdevs. The top of the tree is the root vdev and vdevs in the layer just below the root (either physical or logical) are the top-level vdevs.

As shown in Figure 1, an administrator has flexibility to construct the vdev tree in just about any manner. This flexibility allows for some interesting configurations; some optimal, others not. For example, the configuration in Figure 1 is probably not an optimal one as the top-level vdevs (disk A, mirror, raid-z1) probably operate at different speeds, and certainly have varying redundancy characteristics.

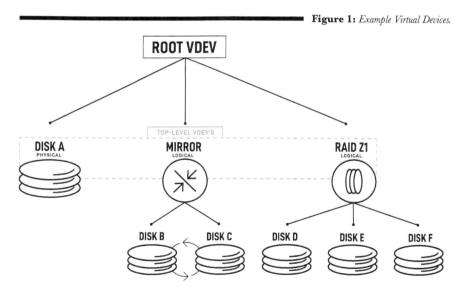

Figure 1: *Example Virtual Devices.*

MIRRORING

Unlike the Logical Volume Manager (LVM) found in Linux, vdevs are not expandable or shrinkable, but provide redundancy by creating a RAID (called RAID-Z in ZFS) or mirrored configuration. When more

15

VIRTUAL DEVICES

than one physical vdev is used to construct a logical vdev, it is possible to configure the logical vdev so the physical vdevs mirror each other. For example, if a logical vdev mirrors two 1TB physical vdevs, the logical vdev has only 1TB of capacity. This is because every byte is stored twice, once on each physical vdev.

Write performance is worse for a mirrored vdev than a single, physical vdev, because each write is written to each physical vdev in the logical vdev. Performance for a given logical vdev is dictated by the slowest child vdev, plus some additional overhead for coordinating the writes.

However, any read made from a mirrored vdev is faster than a single physical vdev because reads are made from two physical vdevs in the mirrored vdev. Therefore, both random and sequential read performance increases as the number of vdevs in a mirror increases.

While mirroring does not increase capacity or write performance, it does increase read performance and provides redundancy. Mirroring your vdevs provides redundancy by duplicating the data. Without mirroring (or RAID-Z as we will see later), if a single device fails, the entire zpool fails. When mirroring N devices, up to N-1 devices can fail, and the system will still operate as normal. However, it is good practice to replace a failed device as quickly as possible as devices often fail in groups, especially if purchased at around the same time.

RAID-Z

If mirroring allows for improved read performance, and allows for the failure of up to N-1 devices in a vdev, why is there a need for a more complex vdev configuration? The answer is simple: money! While a mirrored configuration provides the best redundancy and improved read performance, it is at the cost of adding more devices and not growing the capacity of the vdev. When a third or fourth device is added to a mirrored vdev, the capacity of the vdev does not grow. Money is then spent on redundancy, not capacity. To get a balance between capacity and redundancy, RAID-Z is the answer.

RAID-Z comes in three configurations: RAID-Z1, RAID-Z2, and RAID-Z3. The only difference between the various flavors is the number of devices that can fail while the vdev remains functional. In a RAID-ZN configuration, N devices can fail and the vdev is still serviceable. With each increasing RAID-Z configuration, an additional device is devoted to redundancy or parity.

RAID-Z works by striping data across some of the devices and then writing a parity block to the remaining devices. RAID-Z1, for example, requires at least three devices for which data is striped across two of the devices, and parity is written to the third. It is worth mentioning that a single device is never used exclusively for parity or data, as both parity and data are spread across the devices.

RAID-Z1 is akin to RAID5, but RAID-Z1 does not suffer from the "write hole" problem typically associated with RAID5 (also RAID1 and RAID6). A "write hole" occurs when the system crashes during a write using RAID1, RAID5, or RAID6. The system is unable to identify which blocks (data or parity) are the correct ones. The system simply knows that parity does not match the data. Therefore, the array creates a "hole." Because of checksumming and ZFS's copy-on-write feature, a crash during a write never causes a "hole" in the data.

RAID-Z2 and RAID-Z3 add additional devices for parity, further extending the redundancy of the vdev. With RAID-Z2, at least four devices are required: two for striping data, and two for parity. RAID-Z3 requires at least five devices: two for striping data, and three for parity.

VIRTUAL DEVICES

As expected, a degradation in speed is associated with an increase in the number of parity drives.

RAID-Z solves the problem associated with a mirrored configuration, that adding more devices does not increase the capacity. With RAID-Z, an increase in the number of devices also increases the capacity of the associated vdev, because additional devices are devoted to striping data not redundancy like when mirroring. It should be noted that you cannot add devices to an existing RAID-Z vdev; only vdevs to a zpool. This is usually sufficient to increase the required storage or redundancy.

PERFORMANCE

While the tradeoffs between redundancy and storage have been explored, the tradeoffs between the different vdev configurations and related performance have not. Before discussing performance, how information is spread across the top-level vdevs requires discussion. The root vdev is responsible for distributing data across the top-level vdevs. The root vdev uses a basic round-robin approach to spreading data across vdevs. This is akin to striping in a typical RAID configuration. However, when adding a vdev to a root vdev, the root vdev is smart enough to start filling the new vdev first, so its used space is equal to that of other top-level vdevs.

Think of a root vdev as an LVM always configured as RAID0. Thus, creating a RAID10 configuration is as easy as creating two vdevs that are configured to mirror each other. The root vdev stripes data across the two vdevs, with each vdev configured to mirror providing the redundancy. This is the same configuration as found in RAID10.

Table 1 below assesses the performance of reads and writes to the root vdev for various configurations. We assume physical vdevs are 1TB in size that can perform 100 IOPS for both reading and writing.

Redundancy is the maximum number of drives that can fail, while the system remains operational.

Table 1: *Performance of vdev configurations.*

CONFIGURATION	DEVICES	CAPACITY (TB)	REDUNDANCY	READ IOPS	WRITE IOPS
1 Striped	1	1	0	100	100
2 Striped	2	2	0	200	200
2 Mirrored	2	1	1	200	100
3 Mirrored	3	1	2	300	100
RAID-Z1	3	2	1	200	200
RAID-Z1	4	3	1	300	300
RAID-Z2	4	2	2	200	200
RAID-Z2	5	3	2	300	300
RAID-Z3	5	2	3	200	200
RAID-Z3	6	3	3	300	300
2 x 1 Striped	2	2	0	200	200
2 x 2 Striped	4	4	0	400	400
2 x 2 Mirrored	4	2	1/vdev	400	200
2 x 3 Mirrored	6	2	1/vdev	600	200
2 x 3 RAID-Z1	6	4	1/vdev	400	400
2 x 4 RAID-Z1	8	6	1/vdev	600	600
2 x 4 RAID-Z2	8	4	2/vdev	400	400
2 x 5 RAID-Z2	10	6	2/vdev	600	600
2 x 5 RAID-Z3	10	4	3/vdev	400	400
2 x 6 RAID-Z3	12	6	3/vdev	600	600

SLOG AND L2ARC

While most of the vdevs have the same purpose, to ultimately store filesystem data, there are two special vdevs configured in ZFS: Separate Log (SLOG) and Level-2 Adaptive Replacement Cache (L2ARC).

VIRTUAL DEVICES

These two vdevs are not directly responsible for storing filesystem data, but instead record changes to the filesystem and cache data.

Because ZFS is a copy-on-write system, if single updates (e.g., writing 300 bytes to a file) are performed immediately, the resulting system is horribly slow. For each write, a number of blocks on the disk require updating. The update includes reading the old block, modifying it in memory, and then writing the new block out to a new location. Any block that references this updated block also requires similar updates. The chain of updates continues all the way up to the uberblock. The ZFS intent log (ZIL) prevents ZFS performance bottlenecks by allowing ZFS to batch changes together. Chapter 4, Filesystem, discusses the ZIL in more detail. This section simply focuses on where the ZIL is stored, and not its purpose.

An option to consider is the creation of a separate vdev for the ZIL called a SLOG, or separate log. This vdev is typically backed by faster media than the rest of the vdevs; often an SSD. Writes to ZFS appear to occur at almost SSD speed, but are persisted to potentially much slower spinning disks. Ultimately, the ZIL is a buffer and buffers are not magic. If the stream of changes written to the ZIL overflows the buffer, the actual storage medium is used and the system slows down. Creating a SLOG on an SSD smooths out bursts of writes, and provides a huge performance improvement.

It is noteworthy that the vdev for a ZIL is the same as all other vdevs. Rather than trusting your SSD to persist data correctly through a crash or worrying that general wear and tear will cause an issue, create a mirrored vdev to offset concerns. This provides redundant copies of the ZIL, but at SSD speed.

A similar performance enhancement is provided by ZFS's caching layer, the adaptive replacement cache or ARC. The ARC caches data blocks in memory for fast access. Chapter 4, ZFS Filesystem, discusses ARC in detail. To provide an even larger cache, without the expense of increasing memory in the system, create a Level-2 ARC (L2ARC) by using a special vdev. The L2ARC vdev, typically backed by fast storage such as SSD, is like the SLOG vdev. Because the L2ARC is only a cache, mirroring is pointless for this vdev. While the SLOG provides write performance improvements, the L2ARC provides read performance improvements.

CHAPTER 3

ZFS Pools

ZFS POOLS

The next layer in the ZFS stack is the ZFS pool, or zpool. The zpool is the layer where the line blurs between filesystem and volume manager. A number of the features found in the zpool are in either a volume manager or a filesystem. For example, a volume manager is usually responsible for growing capacity; whereas, checksumming data is normally done in a filesystem. In ZFS, the zpool layer handles both features. Figure 2 shows how a zpool is constructed from vdevs.

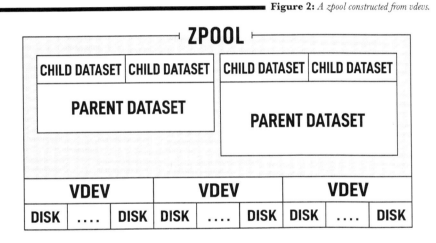

Figure 2: *A zpool constructed from vdevs.*

STRIPES

A traditional volume manager manages devices with fixed-size blocks, and provides a fixed number of these blocks to a filesystem. Volume managers can increase (or decrease) the number of blocks exposed to a filesystem, but this requires orchestration with the target filesystem, and any other filesystems using that volume or device.

In ZFS, blocks are called stripes because they are striped across all vdevs that make up the zpool. The size of a stripe changes dynamically based upon the number of vdevs used and the workload of the dataset (filesystem). The default size of a stripe in ZFS is 128KB, but can grow to as large as 1MB.

Vdevs are added to or removed from a zpool to change the zpool capacity. Unlike other systems, available space in a zpool is equally accessible to all filesystems attached to it. There is no need to grow one filesystem and shrink another; all space in a zpool is shared.

ZFS OBJECT TREE

The zpool is simply a tree of objects of various types. The root node of the zpool tree is the uberblock. The uberblock points to a root block pointer. The root block pointer points to a meta_dnode, which in turn, points to an array of meta-objects. The array of meta-objects for a given zpool is the meta-object set (MOS). The MOS contains meta-objects of various types, including filesystems, snapshots, ZVOLs, and clones. A special, space map object is always included in the array. The space map contains all the used and free blocks in the zpool. Each meta-object contains a pointer to another node in the tree that describes that particular meta-object type. Figure 3 shows a zpool, its MOS layer, and an object set containing the objects that make up a filesystem.

Figure 3: *MOS and object set layers.*

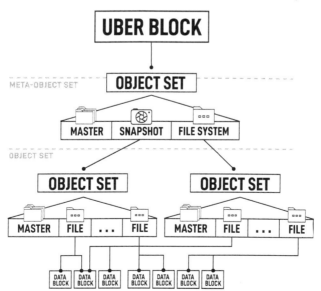

ZFS POOLS

For reference, the various types of objects in ZFS are noted in Table 2. Most of these object types are not discussed in this book, and are only important for ZFS developers, but are provided for the curious administrator.

Table 2: *ZFS object types.*

TYPE	DESCRIPTION
NONE	Unallocated object.
OBJECT_DIRECTORY	DSL object directory ZFS Attribute Processor object.
OBJECT_ARRAY	Object used to store an array of object numbers.
PACKED_NVLIST	Packed nvlist object.
SPACE_MAP	Storage Pool Allocator disk block usage list.
INTENT_LOG	Intent Log.
DNODE	Object of dnodes (metadnode).
OBJSET	Collection of objects.
DSL_DATASET_CHILD_MAP	DSL ZAP object containing child DSL directory information.
DSL_OBJSET_SNAP_MAP	DSL ZAP object containing snapshot information for a dataset.
DSL_PROPS	DSL ZAP properties object containing properties for a DSL dir object.
BPLIST	Block pointer list – used to store the "deadlist": list of block pointers deleted since the last snapshot, and the "deferred free list" used for sync to convergence.
BPLIST_HDR	BPLIST header: stores the bplist_phys_t structure.
ACL	ACL (Access Control List) object.
PLAIN_FILE	ZPL Plain file.
DIRECTORY_CONTENTS	ZPL Directory ZAP Object.
MASTER_NODE	ZPL Master Node ZAP object: head object used to identify root directory, delete queue, and version for a filesystem.
DELETE_QUEUE	The delete queue provides a list of deletes that were in-progress when the filesystem was force unmounted or because of a system failure such as a power outage. Upon the next mount of the filesystem, the delete queue is processed to remove files/dirs in the delete queue. This mechanism avoids leaking files and directories in the filesystem.

Table 2: *ZFS object types.*

TYPE	DESCRIPTION
ZVOL	ZFS Volume (ZVOL).
ZVOL_PROP	ZVOL properties.

DNODES

The Data Management Unit (DMU) is responsible for consuming blocks from vdevs and grouping them into objects. Objects are defined by a 512 byte structure called a dnode. Dnodes are similar to inodes in other filesystems, such as ext2/3/4, found in Linux. While there are various fields in a dnode, this book only covers the following:

- **type**- Indicates the type of object described by the dnode.

- **nblkptr**- A number containing the number of block pointers referenced by the dnode. The number of block pointers is set at object creation and is never changed.

- **blkptr**- A variable length field that contains 1 to 3 block pointers.

- **nlevels**- The number of levels of indirection for an object.

Unlike inodes, that use the last few pointers in the structure to reference multiple levels of indirection, a dnode always has the same number of levels of indirection. When an object is created, a single, direct block pointer points at the data. A second level of indirection is created when the object grows larger than 128K. The single block pointer then points to a 16KB indirect block pointer that contains 128 block pointers. If an object grows even larger, another level of indirection is created and pointers are updated appropriately. To ensure consistency, a 256-bit checksum is computed for all of the data pointed to by a block pointer.

ZFS POOLS

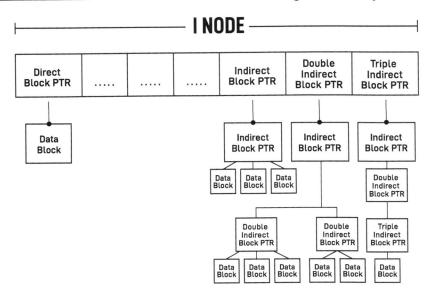

Figure 4: *Inode block pointer structure.*

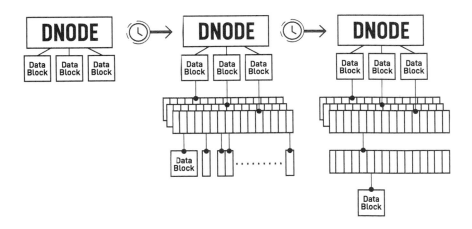

Figure 5: *A dnode as a file grows.*

CONSISTENCY

Beyond the flexibility of ZFS, the consistency provided by ZFS is one of the main reasons for the popularity of ZFS. Writes never leave the system in an inconsistent state. To achieve this, ZFS leverages a list of uberblocks, always caching at least 31 previous uberblocks for recovery. When a zpool is created, 128KBs within it are allocated for uberblocks. A physical vdev with 512-byte sectors, creates 128 uberblocks. A physical vdev with 4KB sectors, creates only 32 uberblocks. Uberblocks are used in sequence as the underlying pool changes. When the allocated uberblocks are exhausted, the sequence starts over forming a ring of uberblocks.

All writes are conducted within transaction groups. A transaction group is a batch of changes made to the system. Each transaction group is numbered with a monotonically increasing 64-bit number. Each transaction group is associated with an uberblock, and the uberblock is written last. This way in-progress changes are not fully committed until the uberblock is fully written. Once an uberblock is written, all other changes in the transaction group have already been written. ZFS can identify the current uberblock by looking for the highest transaction number. This system of writing the changes in a transaction group first, then updating the uberblock ensures that system integrity always remains intact, even in the event of a failure.

ZFS ATTRIBUTE PROCESSOR

The ZFS Attribute Processor (ZAP) works with the DMU to process special objects called ZAP objects. The ZAP module that manages these objects is an on-disk hash table with overflow lists that contains name/value pairs. ZAP objects are used for storing directory entries, and other metadata.

A directory in ZFS is created by pointing a dnode at a ZAP object. The name/values in the ZAP object map file names to object numbers. The object numbers are the index into the objset dnode that points to the object location on the disk. The hash table in the ZAP object allows for fast lookup, insertion, deletion, and full scanning of the directory. Given the flexible nature of ZAP objects, simply a name/value hash table, ZAP objects also store other metadata, such as property lists.

There are two main types of ZAP objects: micro ZAP and fat ZAP. A microZAP object is one block (up to 128K) and contains simple attributes (64-bit number) with names limited to 50 bytes in length. Whereas, fat ZAP objects are a full object in ZFS that hash into a pointer table which points at name/value storage allowing for the storage of larger name/value pairs. (Ref: http://www.osdevcon.org/2009/slides/zfs_internals_uli_graef.pdf)

ZFS POSIX LAYER

The ZFS POSIX Layer (ZPL) provides POSIX-semantics for the ZFS filesystem. When a dnode describes a filesystem object such as a file or directory, a znode is embedded in the dnode. This znode contains all metadata needed to provide POSIX-semantics to the Linux kernel. As explained above, directories are stored in ZAP objects and files are DMU objects.

Whenever a process performs a read or write to a file, the call is passed through the ZPL module. The module is responsible for dispatching the call to the ZIL, DMU, or ZAP appropriately. Newly written data is dispatched to the ZIL so that it is properly persisted. Reading data is done via the DMU (or possibly ZIL). Finally, the ZAP conducts directory reading and writing.

SNAPSHOTS AND CLONES

Beyond filesystems, the MOS layer in the zpool is responsible for snapshots and clones. A snapshot provides a point-in-time, read-only view of the state of the filesystem. A clone is a copy of the filesystem. Both snapshots and clones leverage the fact that ZFS is a copy-on-write system; data is never overwritten during an update, instead a copy is made and referenced in the tree. Because of this, the zpool uses only slightly more than 1TB of space in a cloned 1TB filesystem. The opposite is true when deleting files. The blocks that contain a freshly deleted file's data are not removed if referenced in a snapshot. Therefore, when deleting a file in ZFS, there is a solid chance that the amount of space used by the vdev does not decrease.

Copying the top-level meta-object in the zpool creates snapshots and clones. Creating a snapshot or clone is virtually instantaneous because only a single block is copied. What was the live filesystem meta-object now becomes the snapshot or clone meta-object. A new meta-object is created for the filesystem that points to old data blocks. When a file is created, updated, or deleted in the live filesystem, new blocks are created or disconnected from the top-level meta-object that describes the filesystem.

CHAPTER 4

ZFS Filesystem

ZFS FILESYSTEM

As mentioned in Chapter 3, ZFS Pools, ZFS blurs the line between volume manager and filesystem. This chapter focuses solely on the functions and features typically found in a traditional filesystem. For reference, Chapter 6, Working with vdevs, describes zpool features such as snapshots and clones, usually found in a volume manager.

CHECKPOINTS

The ZFS filesystem operates by creating a series of checkpoints. A checkpoint is a group of changes that have occurred since the last checkpoint was committed to disk. Checkpoints occur either every 5 seconds, when 64MB of changes have accumulated, or an administrative action, such as a snapshot, forces a checkpoint. (These values are tunable. For more information, refer to Chapter 9, Performance Tuning.) The group of changes that occur between checkpoints is called a transaction group. The number of changes in a transaction group is variable. Because ZFS does not overwrite blocks, any writes to the filesystem between checkpoints are stored in the ZIL. More on the ZIL in Chapter 6, Working with vdevs.

The ZFS filesystem always remains in a consistent state because a checkpoint is not considered committed until a new uberblock is created. If the system crashes while all changes in the transaction group are committing to disk, the system restarts and reads the uberblock with the highest transaction group ID. In such a crash scenario, that uberblock, and all associated child blocks will not have changed. It will appear as if the changes in that transaction group never occurred. There is no need to replay a journal or check the filesystem to ensure lack of corruption. What about the changes made after the last checkpoint? This is where the ZIL enters the picture.

ZFS INTENT LOG

When a change occurs, such as writing 300 bytes into the middle of a file, the write is not flushed to disk immediately. Instead, ZFS stores this change in the ZIL. The ZIL records all changes to the filesystem: writes, permission changes, symbolic links, new directories, etc. Unlike traditional filesystems that keep a journal to enable filesystem restoration to a consistent state after a crash, ZFS uses the ZIL only to track changes between checkpoints. After a crash, ZFS forces a checkpoint by committing all changes in the ZIL to disk. This way data that the ZFS filesystem committed to persisting is not lost, and performing a lengthy filesystem check is not necessary to ensure lack of corruption.

Writing data to the ZIL and then to the filesystem itself is an expensive process. To improve performance, data blocks are allocated on the device and their location is stored in the ZIL. When a checkpoint occurs, the meta-objects simply point to these allocated data blocks. This way data is only written once.

To further improve performance, when a program calls `fsync`, a checkpoint is not created. Instead, all data is flushed from a cache to the ZIL. Forcing a checkpoint with every `fsync` call is extremely costly, especially for programs like databases that often call `fsync` after each write.

Another performance improvement provided by the ZIL is the ability to squash conflicting commits. For example, if the user were to create the directory my_files and then immediately delete the directory before ZFS created a checkpoint, it is possible to squash this change. The same is true for permission changes, and data written to disk. A database is

ZFS FILESYSTEM

another great example of squashable changes. Multiple updates to the same record in a database are not written, only the resulting record after all the changes are made is written to disk.

WRITING DATA

To provide a concrete understanding of how ZFS operates, the steps required to write data during a checkpoint to an existing file are enumerated below. These steps provide a medium-level overview of how writing data works. However, there are numerous idiosyncrasies (new files, files that need additional indirection, etc.) not covered here.

1. Allocate and write any new blocks to disk. If the write is in the middle of a file (i.e., overwriting data), then the data blocks are written to a new location because ZFS never overwrites data.

2. Add the pointer to the new data block to the indirect block. Again, because ZFS never overwrites anything, a new indirect block is created with the new pointers and is written to disk. This requires that the pointer to this new indirect block be updated as well. This process of creating new indirect blocks, writing them to new locations, and updating the parent indirect block occurs all the way up to the dnode.

3. Create a new dnode with the new indirect block pointer and updated file size (assuming the file grew). This dnode is written to a new location as well. Update parent dnodes that reference this dnode in a similar fashion.

4. Continue this updating from leaf to root in the filesystem tree within the MOS layer in the zpool.

5. Allocate a new uberblock to the new transaction group ID once all changes are propagated up the tree. Then write this new uberblock to the next available slot in the list of uberblocks within the zpool.

Any time a dnode or indirect block needs updating, it is first read from disk into memory. All updates occur in memory, and these blocks are written to a new location on the disk only when all changes have occurred. This prevents having to read and write the same dnode or indirect block to and from the disk multiple times. Also, by only modifying an in-memory copy of the dnode or indirect block, conflicting changes (e.g., adding then removing a directory) are squashed.

ARC AND L2ARC CACHE

Because ZFS never overwrites blocks, the astute reader will notice that reads from ZFS are typically random. While suitable for SSDs, ZFS's goal is to support storage mediums with any read and write characteristics well. This is achieved via a caching layer. Blocks (including dnodes, indirect blocks, data blocks, etc.) are cached in an ARC.

ZFS's ARC is an improvement upon least recently used (LRU) cache, including Linux's LRU 2Q cache. The ARC also uses two lists, L1 and L2, of variable size. The two lists operate as LRU lists where L1 contains pages seen only once recently, and L2 contains pages seen at least twice recently. The two lists and how pages flow between them can be seen in Figure 6. The ARC uses the following replacement policy: replace the LRU page in L1, if L1 contains exactly $c/2$ (where c is the size of the cache) pages; otherwise, replace the LRU page in L2. Pages flow through the two lists in the cache via the following algorithm:

> If the page is in L1 or L2, move the page to the top of L2
>
> Otherwise;
>
>> If L1 has exactly c/2 pages, remove the page on the bottom of L1 and insert the new page at the top of L1.
>>
>> Otherwise, if the cache is full ($|L1| + |L2| = c$), remove the page at the bottom of L2. Insert the page at the top of L1.

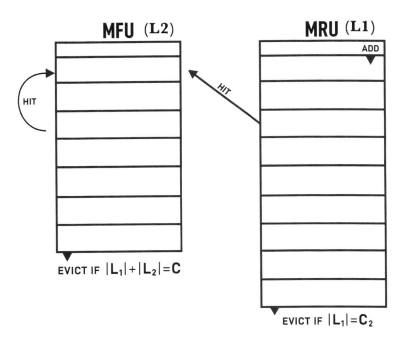

Figure 6: *ARC page lists.*

While the ARC in ZFS is constrained by the amount of RAM on the machine, there is a second level cache available, appropriately named L2ARC. The L2ARC typically resides on an SSD or similar fast storage to improve performance (in fact, using spinning disk hardly improves performance, if at all). This on-disk cache works in the same fashion as RAM based ARC. When a page is ready for eviction from the ARC, it is sent to the L2ARC. When a page is ready for eviction from the L2ARC, it is first evicted and then removed from both levels of cache.

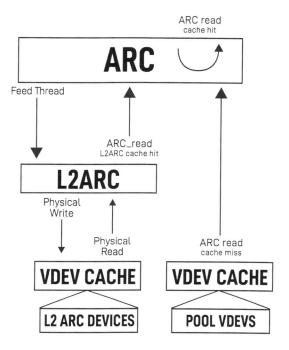

Figure 7: *ARC and L2ARC.*

Linux also employs a page cache in the Virtual File System (VFS) layer, and throughout the kernel to improve performance. The Linux cache uses a modified version of an LRU based cache policy, LRU 2Q. The LRU 2Q policy is not directly implemented as found in the academic paper, but instead simplified. At a high level, the cache has two lists of pages: `active_list` and `inactive_list`, as show in Figure 7. When first allocating a page, it is placed on the `inactive_list` that operates like a FIFO queue. If the page is used again while in the `inactive_list`, it is moved to the `active_list`. When a page reaches the bottom of the `active_list` a referenced flag is checked. The flag gets set whenever the page is referenced. If the flag is not set, the page moves to the `inactive_`

ZFS FILESYSTEM

list. If the flag is set, then it is cleared and moves the page to the top of the list checking the next page. Linux further modifies the LRU 2Q policy by always maintaining the `active_list` at 2/3 the size of the total page cache. The `inactive_list` pages are ultimately evicted.

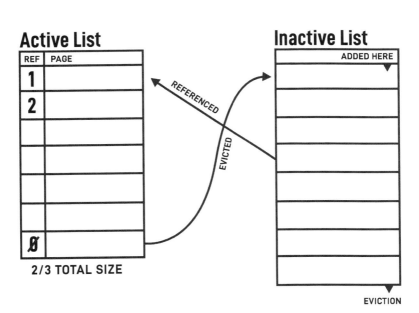

Figure 8: *Linux cache page lists.*

Unfortunately, this causes double-caching when ZFS is used on Linux. Data is cached both in the Linux page cache, and in ZFS's ARC. While the performance impact is minimal, it can greatly increase the amount of memory used by the system. Although it is not possible to disable Linux's page cache, it is possible to tune ZFS's ARC to prevent much of this double-caching. See Chapter 9, Performance and Tuning, for ways to tune the performance of ZFS and possibly save memory.

ZFS PROPERTIES

Nearly every configurable parameter in ZFS is configured via a property. Properties apply to both zpools and datasets, but are discussed here as there are almost twice as many dataset properties as zpool properties. A complete list of zpool properties is available using the `zpool utility` and the get command: `zpool get all`. Some of the properties are read-only, some are configurable only when the zpool is created, and others are changeable at any time. Table 3 enumerates the properties for a zpool and when they can be changed, if at all. Detailed information for each property can be found in the `zpool utility` man page.

Table 3: zpool properties.

NAME	VALUE TYPE	CONFIGURABLE
ALLOCATED	Number	Read-only
ALTROOT	String	At creation
ASHIFT	Number	At creation
AUTOEXPAND	Boolean	At creation
AUTOREPLACE	Boolean	At creation
BOOTFS	Boolean	At creation
CACHEFILE	String	At creation
CAPACITY	Number	Read-only
COMMENT	String	At creation
DEDUPDITTO	Number	At creation
DEDUPRATIO	Number	Read-only
DELEGATION	Boolean	At creation
EXPANDSIZE	Number	Read-only
FAILMODE	String	At creation

ZFS FILESYSTEM

Table 3: zpool properties.

NAME	VALUE TYPE	CONFIGURABLE
FRAGMENTATION	Number	Read-only
FREE	String	Read-only
FREEING	Number	Read-only
GUID	String	Read-only
HEALTH	String	Read-only
LEAKED	Number	Read-only
LISTSNAPSHOTS	String	At creation
READONLY	Boolean	At creation
SIZE	Number	Read-only
VERSION	Number	At creation

Datasets also have properties that allow configuring how the dataset operates, and to read information about the dataset. Table 4 lists the properties associated with datasets. For detailed information about each property, see the man page for the `zfs utility`.

Table 4: dataset properties.

NAME	VALUE TYPE	CONFIGURABLE
ACLINHERIT	String	Configurable
ACLTYPE	String	Configurable
ATIME	Boolean	Configurable
AVAILABLE	Number	Read-only
CANMOUNT	String	Configurable
CASESENSITIVITY	String	At creation
CHECKSUM	String	Configurable
CLONES	String	Read-only

Table 4: dataset properties.

NAME	VALUE TYPE	CONFIGURABLE
COMPRESSION	String	Configurable
COMPRESSRATIO	Number	Read-only
CONTEXT*	String	Configurable
COPIES	Number	Configurable
CREATION	String	Read-only
DEDUP	String	Configurable
DEFCONTEXT*	String	Configurable
DEFER_DESTROY	Boolean	Read-only
DEVICES	Boolean	Configurable
DNODESIZE	String	Configurable
EXEC	Boolean	Configurable
FILESYSTEM_COUNT	Number	Read-only
FILESYSTEM_LIMIT	Number	Configurable
FSCONTEXT*	String	Configurable
LOGBIAS	String	Configurable
LOGICALREFERENCED	Number	Read-only
LOGICALUSED	Number	Read-only
MLSLABEL	String	Configurable
MOUNTED	Boolean	Read-only
MOUNTPOINT	String	Configurable
NBMAND	Boolean	Configurable
NORMALIZATION	String	At creation
ORIGIN	String	Read-only
OVERLAY*	String	Configurable

ZFS FILESYSTEM

Table 4: dataset properties.

NAME	VALUE TYPE	CONFIGURABLE
PRIMARYCACHE	String	Configurable
QUOTA	Number	Configurable
READONLY	Boolean	Configurable
RECEIVE_RESUME_TOKEN	String (opaque)	Read-only
RECORDSIZE	Number	Configurable
REDUNDANT_METADATA	String	Configurable
REFCOMPRESSRATIO	Number	Read-only
REFERENCED	Number	Read-only
REFQUOTA	Number	Configurable
REFRESERVATION	Number	Configurable
RELATIME	Boolean	Configurable
RESERVATION	Number	Configurable
ROOTCONTEXT*	String	Configurable
SECONDARYCACHE	String	Configurable
SETUID	Boolean	Configurable
SHARENFS	Boolean	Configurable
SHARESMB	Boolean	Configurable
SNAPDEV	String	Configurable
SNAPDIR	String	Configurable
SNAPSHOT_COUNT	Number	Read-only
SNAPSHOT_LIMIT	Number	Configurable
SYNC	String	Configurable
TYPE	String	Read-only
USED	Number	Read-only

Table 4: dataset properties.

NAME	VALUE TYPE	CONFIGURABLE
USEDBYCHILDREN	Number	Read-only
USEDBYDATASET	Number	Read-only
USEDBYREFRESERVATION	Number	Read-only
USEDBYSNAPSHOTS	Number	Read-only
USERREFS	Number	Read-only
UTF8ONLY	Boolean	At creation
VERSION	String	Configurable
VOLBLOCKSIZE	Number	Read-only
VOLSIZE	Number	Configurable
VSCAN	Boolean	Configurable
WRITTEN	Number	Read-only
XATTR	String	Configurable
ZONED	Boolean	Configurable

*Properties are only used with SELinux.

Some properties do not immediately take effect when set. For example, setting the compression property on a filesystem does not cause ZFS to traverse through the files in the filesystem and compress them. Instead, any new files written are compressed. To obtain the effect of compressing the entire filesystem, the ZFS method of "send and receive" from one filesystem to another can be used. For more information on sending and receiving ZFS filesystems, see Chapter 8, Advanced Filesystem Features.

CHAPTER 5

Native ZFS Encryption

NATIVE ZFS ENCRYPTION

A BRIEF OVERVIEW OF ENCRYPTION

Encryption has three general categories: encryption in transit, encryption at rest, and encryption in use. This section focuses on encryption at rest, as that is what most pertains to ZFS. However, data sitting on a disk is read, so encryption in use is also important. Encryption in use applies when an attacker can monitor an application's data in memory. This is one of the most difficult kinds of attacks to protect against and usually requires encryption support built into both the operating system and the physical RAM the machine is using.

Encrypting data at rest protects against an attacker who can read from (and possibly write to) a disk containing private information. The attacker may be someone who has physically stolen either the hard drives or the entire system, an attacker who has managed to gain root privileges on the system, or even a legitimate user who has root privileges. Permissions do not provide adequate protection against these kinds of attacks. File and disk level encryption can mitigate these attacks. The new encryption feature in ZFS protects against these kinds of attacks by encrypting the entire dataset.

Before talking about how encryption is implemented in ZFS, it is important to have a basic understanding of symmetric encryption. This section does not provide a complete and comprehensive explanation of encryption, but delivers a basic understanding.

Encryption is the process of taking sensitive data, called plaintext, and transforming it into indecipherable, pseudorandom data, called ciphertext. Ciphertext can only be decrypted back into plaintext with a secret key. An attacker attempting to read ciphertext without the key cannot determine useful information about the plaintext (except perhaps the size). Symmetric encryption involves a single secret key (usually between 16 and 32 bytes long) that is used to encrypt and decrypt the data.

Symmetric encryption is often implemented by a block cipher. A block cipher takes one block of plaintext and the secret key as input, and generates one block of ciphertext as output. The most common block cipher in use today is the Advanced Encryption Standard or AES. AES is so common that modern x86_64 Intel CPUs have accelerated AES instructions built into the hardware.

AES, like all block ciphers, is limited because it can only encrypt a single block of plaintext with a single call. To allow the encryption of arbitrary amounts of data, AES needs to be applied to all the plaintext blocks. The way in which AES is applied is called the mode of operation. The simplest mode of operation, known as the electronic code book (ECB) mode, is to iterate over the entire plaintext, one block at a time, and apply the block cipher independently to each block (Figure 8). This accomplishes the goal of allowing encryption of more than a single block of plaintext at a time, but there is a significant problem. Because each block of plaintext is encrypted in the same way and using the same block cipher, equivalent input blocks result in an equivalent ciphertext block. This allows an attacker to find sensitive patterns in the data. Thus, real-world encryption applications do not use ECB.

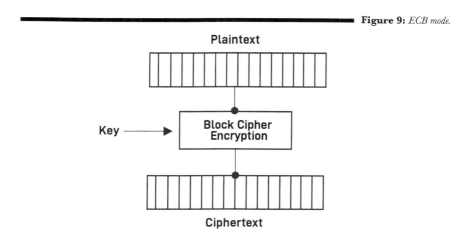

Figure 9: *ECB mode.*

NATIVE ZFS ENCRYPTION

To ensure a system is secure, it must be assured that the ciphertext cannot be modified without being detected. To ensure the ciphertext has not been modified, a Message Authentication Code, or MAC, is computed. A MAC is a cryptographic checksum. Unlike a conventional checksum, a MAC requires a secret key. A MAC can only be generated and verify if the secret key is known. Thus, the ciphertext cannot be modified without also modifying the MAC, which can only be done if the secret key is known. Today, many modern encryption modes such as GCM (Galois/Counter Mode) and CCM (Counter with CBC-MAC) produce a MAC. These modes are called Authenticated Encryption modes, and ZFS uses these authenticated encryption modes exclusively.

ADVANTAGES OF NATIVE ZFS ENCRYPTION

Native ZFS encryption in Linux provides several advantages over other disk-based encryption solutions such as those provided by LUKS and dm-crypt. LUKS and dm-crypt work by encrypting each block of data written to disk. The problem is that there is no way to store additional encryption metadata like the MAC without destroying the alignment of blocks on-disk, separating the metadata from the encrypted blocks, or creating a lot of unused space. Block devices are only meant to be read in constant sized and aligned blocks (usually of 512 bytes). Encryption algorithms, such as AES-XTS, do not provide a MAC rendering them unauthenticated.

Attempting to put ZFS on top of a disk-based-encryption solution like LUKS or dm-crypt presents a few problems. By default, ZFS always stores multiple copies of metadata and can store multiple copies of user data, depending upon the configuration. Doing so incurs unnecessary CPU overhead. Another problem is that the zpool is completely unreadable until the keys are provided. Linux is not able to recognize that a filesystem belongs to a zpool until it is decrypted. Useful administrative functions such as zpool scrubs and resilvers do not function without entering the user's keys and decrypting the data. With native ZFS encryption, scrubs, and resilvers can occur on encrypted zpools. Using LUKS or dm-crypt also makes it impossible to have multiple datasets encrypted with different keys.

Using an encrypted filesystem, such as ecryptfs, on a ZFS volume presents other problems. Encrypted filesystems hook into the POSIX read and write calls to decrypt and encrypt data. As data is written, extra space in between the blocks is added to store encryption metadata. The space is transparently allocated and deallocated as the file is read from disk. Encrypted filesystems may not support encrypting file metadata such as file names, owner and group, permissions bits, and extended attributes; or may require special handling to add these features. In addition, the extra space for the metadata can offset the alignment of file blocks. This can lead to significant performance degradation, particularly in databases and virtual machines. Furthermore, encrypted filesystems prevent ZFS from compressing data. This is because ZFS only ever reads and writes encrypted blocks. Encrypted data is pseudorandom which cannot be easily compressed.

IMPLEMENTATION

ZFS encryption works by exploiting ZFS's existing block pointer-based on-disk format. The encryption metadata for user data is stored in the block pointer. This does not impact performance because ZFS always reads the block pointer when reading the data from disk. This also means that the metadata can be stored without using any additional space.

NATIVE ZFS ENCRYPTION

Because ZFS functions as both a volume manager and a filesystem, it can intelligently manage when to perform encryption. Recall that using ZFS on a disk-based encryption solution meant that multiple copies of the same data would be encrypted. With ZFS encryption, multiple copies of the same data are encrypted only once, eliminating CPU overhead. Another advantage is that ZFS can apply encryption after compression; providing good compression ratios.

ZFS only encrypts sensitive userdata leaving the pool structure unencrypted so that useful operations, such as scrubs and resilvers, can occur even when the keys are not loaded. The pool can be scrubbed and resilvered because ZFS stores ciphertext checksums. Efficient backups are also possible without the keys using zfs send and zfs recv, although the data is still not readable until the keys are loaded. The system administrator can elect to encrypt different datasets with different user keys, or leave some datasets unencrypted.

CHAPTER 6

Working with vdevs

WORKING WITH VDEVS

Because of ZFS's flexibility in what is considered a physical vdev, files can be used as the physical vdevs in all of the examples. All examples in this book use these six files, each 100MB (made quickly using `fallocate`):

```
# ls -l
total 585972
-rw-r--r-- 1 root root 100000000 Nov  1 21:33 disk1
-rw-r--r-- 1 root root 100000000 Nov  1 21:33 disk2
-rw-r--r-- 1 root root 100000000 Nov  1 21:32 disk3
-rw-r--r-- 1 root root 100000000 Nov  1 21:32 disk4
-rw-r--r-- 1 root root 100000000 Nov  1 21:32 disk5
-rw-r--r-- 1 root root 100000000 Nov  1 21:32 disk6
```

ZPOOL COMMAND BASICS

The `zpool` utility creates and manages **vdevs**. Zpools are also created and managed using the `zpool` utility. This makes sense when you consider that a zpool is simply a collection of top-level vdevs. The first argument to the `zpool` utility is the command or action you want to perform on the pool. More in-depth information about each command can be found in the man pages for the `zpool` utility. A list of each command with a brief description is provided below:

Table 5: zpool commands.

COMMAND	DESCRIPTION
CREATE	Creates new zpool given a list of virtual devices.
DESTROY	Removes zpool.
ADD	Adds vdev to zpool.
REMOVE	Removes vdev from zpool.
LABELCLEAR	Removes ZFS label information from specified device.
LIST	Lists given pools along with health status and usage.
IOSTAT	Displays I/O statistics for given pool.

Table 5: zpool commands.

COMMAND	DESCRIPTION
STATUS	Displays detailed health status for a given pool.
ONLINE	Brings specified physical device online.
OFFLINE	Takes specified physical device offline.
CLEAR	Clears device errors in specified pool.
REOPEN	Reopens all vdevs associated with specified pool.
ATTACH	Attaches new device to existing zpool device.
DETACH	Detaches device from mirror.
REPLACE	Replaces old device with new device in specified pool.
SPLIT	Splits devices off pool creating new pool. (Note: not usable with files.)
SCRUB	Begins scrub, which examines all data of specified pool.
IMPORT	Imports specified pool into system.
EXPORT	Exports given pools from system.
UPGRADE	Displays pools without all supported features enabled and pools formatted using a legacy version of ZFS.
REGUID	Generates new unique identifier for pool.
HISTORY	Displays command history of specified pool.
EVENTS	Displays description of different events generated by kernel.
GET	Retrieves given list of properties for specified pool.
SET	Sets given property on specified pool.

All zpool commands must be run as root.

MIRRORED VDEVS

Use the following command to create a mirrored zpool labeled "redundant" using two of our disk files, as shown here:

WORKING WITH VDEVS

```
# zpool create redundant mirror /home/wspeirs/disk1 \
/home/wspeirs/disk2
```

Note that when using something like a file as a vdev, specify the full path to the file; otherwise, the tool searches /dev for a device with that name. The following two attempts do not work because no path, and a relative path were provided:

```
# zpool create redundant mirror disk1 disk2
cannot open 'disk1': no such device in /dev
must be a full path or shorthand device name

# zpool create redundant mirror ./disk1 ./disk2
cannot open './disk1': no such device in /dev
must be a full path or shorthand device name
```

Pool names must begin with a letter, and can only contain alphanumeric characters as well as underscore, dash, period, colon, and space. Using a dash or space in a pool name is not recommended as it renders output from other commands harder to parse, and input to commands more difficult because of bash (or other shells) interpreting dash and space. Note that, "mirror", "raidz", "spare", and "log" are all reserved names. Also, any name that matches the pattern "c[0-9]*" is a reserved name.

Creating a pool with 3 mirrored devices works exactly as expected, as this example shows:

```
# zpool create redundant mirror /home/wspeirs/disk1 \
/home/wspeirs/disk2 /home/wspeirs/disk3
```

To examine zpools, the `zpool list` command is used. Specify either the name of the desired pool to inspect, or nothing to see all pools, as in these examples:

```
# zpool list
```

NAME	SIZE	ALLOC	FREE	EXPANDSZ	FRAG	CAP	DEDUP	HEALTH	ALTROOT
REDUNDANT	80M	61K	79.9M	-	1%	0%	1.00x	Online	-
REDUNDANT2	80M	50K	80.0M	-	1%	0%	1.00x	Online	-

```
# zpool list redundant
NAME            SIZE   ALLOC   FREE    EXPANDSZ   FRAG   CAP   DEDUP   HEALTH   ALTROOT
REDUNDANT       80M    61K     79.9M      —        1%    0%    1.00x   Online   -
```

While `zpool list` provides a high-level overview of the various zpools on the system, `zpool status` provides a bit more detail about the makeup of the zpool itself. As with `zpool list`, specify it with or without a pool name, as shown here:

```
# zpool status redundant
POOL: redundant
STATE: ONLINE
SCAN: none requested
CONFIG:
    NAME                         STATE     READ   WRITE   CKSUM
    Redundant                    Online    0      0       0
      mirror-0                   Online    0      0       0
        /home/wspeirs/disk1      Online    0      0       0
        /home/wspeirs/disk2      Online    0      0       0
        /home/wspeirs/disk3      Online    0      0       0
ERRORS: No known data errors
```

The command shows all zpools in the system along with their state and the number of read, write, and checksum errors. The mirrored pool redundant shows that all of its devices are online and without errors. The scan line shows the status of a scrub or resilver. If either have completed, the results of the operation are displayed. This pool was never scrubbed or resilvered.

To see information about the I/O status of a zpool, simply use the `zpool iostat` command. Like `list` and `status`, this command either takes a single pool name, or is left blank to see all pools, as in this example:

WORKING WITH VDEVS

```
# zpool iostat
POOL          ALLOC    FREE     READ    WRITE    READ    WRITE
redundant     61K      79.9M    0       0        0       77
redundant2    61K      79.9M    0       0        0       87
```

Notice the difference in bandwidth between these two pools. Redundant is created with three disks; whereas, redundant2 was created with only two disks. This creates a pool with a hierarchy of vdevs.

To create a zpool that mimics the functionality of RAID10, a pair of mirrored vdevs with data striped across them, simply pass back-to-back mirror configurations on the command line, as shown here:

```
# zpool create raid_10 mirror /home/wspeirs/disk1 \
  /home/wspeirs/disk2  mirror /home/wspeirs/disk3 \
  /home/wspeirs/disk4

# zpool status
POOL: raid_10
STATE: ONLINE
SCAN: none requested
CONFIG:
NAME                          STATE    READ    WRITE    CKSUM
raid_10                       Online   0       0        0
  mirror-0                    Online   0       0        0
    /home/wspeirs/disk1       Online   0       0        0
    /home/wspeirs/disk2       Online   0       0        0
  mirror-1                    Online   0       0        0
    /home/wspeirs/disk3       Online   0       0        0
    /home/wspeirs/disk4       Online   0       0        0

ERRORS: No known data errors
```

The command automatically names the mirrored vdevs `mirror-0` and `mirror-1`.

Once a mirrored zpool is created, add additional vdevs to the zpool. Given our example "raid_10" zpool above, let's add disk5 to mirror-0 and disk6 to mirror-1. This increases redundancy by including another vdev in each mirror. The zpool `attach` command does exactly that:

```
# zpool attach raid_10 /home/wspeirs/disk1 /home/wspeirs/disk5
# zpool attach raid_10 /home/wspeirs/disk3 /home/wspeirs/disk6
```

```
# zpool status
POOL: raid_10
STATE: ONLINE
SCAN: none requested
CONFIG:

NAME                         STATE     READ   WRITE   CKSUM
raid_10                      Online    0      0       0
    mirror-0                 Online    0      0       0
        /home/wspeirs/disk1  Online    0      0       0
        /home/wspeirs/disk2  Online    0      0       0
    mirror-1                 Online    0      0       0
        /home/wspeirs/disk3  Online    0      0       0
        /home/wspeirs/disk4  Online    0      0       0
        /home/wspeirs/disk6  Online    0      0       0
ERRORS: No known data errors
```

The first `zpool attach` command added disk5, and the second added disk6 to the configuration. The command works by specifying the pool and an existing vdev that the new vdev should be attached to. The `zpool add` command adds a new vdev to an existing pool. Use this command to grow the size of the raid_10 pool, as in this example:

```
# zpool add raid_10 mirror /home/wspeirs/disk5 \
  /home/wspeirs/disk6
```

WORKING WITH VDEVS

```
# zpool status
POOL: raid_10
STATE: ONLINE
SCAN: resilvered 46.5K in 0h0m with 0 errors on Mon Nov
7 21:13:10 2016
CONFIG:
```

NAME	STATE	READ	WRITE	CKSUM
raid_10	Online	0	0	0
mirror-0	Online	0	0	0
/home/wspeirs/disk1	Online	0	0	0
/home/wspeirs/disk2	Online	0	0	0
mirror-1	Online	0	0	0
/home/wspeirs/disk3	Online	0	0	0
/home/wspeirs/disk4	Online	0	0	0
mirror-2	Online	0	0	0
/home/wspeirs/disk5	Online	0	0	0
/home/wspeirs/disk6	Online	0	0	0

```
errors: no known data errors
```

Use extra care to remove vdevs from zpools using the `zpool detach` command. Because data is striped across all the vdevs in a zpool, removing top-level vdevs would render the pool useless. Here is how to remove a mirror from a vdev:

```
# zpool detach raid_10 /home/wspeirs/disk6
# zpool status
POOL: raid_10
STATE: ONLINE
SCAN: resilvered 46.5K in 0h0m with 0 errors on Mon Nov  7
21:13:10 2016
CONFIG:
```

```
NAME                              STATE   READ  WRITE  CKSUM
raid_10                           Online    0     0      0
    mirror-0                      Online    0     0      0
        /home/wspeirs/disk1       Online    0     0      0
        /home/wspeirs/disk2       Online    0     0      0
    mirror-1                      Online    0     0      0
        /home/wspeirs/disk3       Online    0     0      0
        /home/wspeirs/disk4       Online    0     0      0
        /home/wspeirs/disk5       Online    0     0      0

errors: no known data errors
```

Notice that disk5 was "promoted" to a top-level vdev. With this action, it is not possible to remove it from the zpool:

```
# zpool detach raid_10 /home/wspeirs/disk5
cannot detach /home/wspeirs/disk5: only applicable to mirror
and replacing vdevs
```

RAID-Z

The command for creating a RAID-Z vdev is like creating a mirrored vdev. Instead of specifying mirror for the type, specify the type of RAID-Z desired. At least 3 vdevs are required for RAID-Z1, 4 for RAID-Z2, and 5 for RAID-Z3. Create a RAID-Z1 vdev using our 3 disk files with a label of raid-z1 using the following `zpool` command:

```
# zpool create raid-z1 raidz1 /home/wspeirs/disk1 \
/home/wspeirs/disk2 /home/wspeirs/disk3
```

Note from the `zpool list` command that this configuration leverages the second of the vdevs for storage, and the third for parity/redundancy, providing 200M of space, as shown in this example:

```
# zpool list
NAME      SIZE   ALLOC  FREE  EXPANDSZ  FRAG  CAP  DEDUP  HEALTH  ALTROOT
raid-z1   272M   92M    272M     -       0%   0%   1.00X  ONLINE    -
```

WORKING WITH VDEVS

When creating vdevs using RAID-Z provide same size vdevs. Failure to do so results in an error from the `zpool` command, similar to this example:

```
# zpool create raid-z1-2 raidz1 /home/wspeirs/disk4 \
  /home/wspeirs/disk5 /home/wspeirs/bigger_disk
invalid vdev specification
use '-f' to override the following errors:
raidz contains devices of different sizes\
```

Unlike mirrored vdevs, it is not possible to add and remove devices to RAID-Z vdevs. Specify all devices upfront when creating a RAID-Z vdev. To create a RAID-Z2 vdev use the following command:

```
# zpool create my-raid-z2 raidz2 /home/wspeirs/disk1 \
  /home/wspeirs/disk2 /home/wspeirs/disk3 /home/wspeirs/disk4
```

Attempting to add another disk, disk5, to the vdev results in the following error message:

```
# zpool attach my-raid-z2 /home/wspeirs/disk1 /home/wspeirs/
disk5 cannot attach /home/wspeirs/disk5 to /home/wspeirs/
disk1: can only attach to mirrors and top-level disks
```

Adding a device to the zpool creates an unmaintainable zpool because one of the top-level vdevs has redundancy, and the other does not.

SLOG AND L2ARC VDEVS

There are two possible, special vdevs to add to a zpool: SLOG/SIL and L2ARC. These two vdevs do not provide or increase storage capacity. Instead, they increase performance by moving the ZIL to a more performant device, and by providing a second layer to the ARC. Chapter 2, Virtual Devices, contains more information about the L2ARC.

When a zpool is created an implicit ZIL is created as well on the provided devices. This is typically created on slower but cheaper devices. To improve performance, use a faster device such as an SSD or some other type of persistent fast storage to store the ZIL. Use the following command to add a fast device fast_disk to a vdev labeled my-raid-z2 as the SLOG/SIL for that zpool:

```
# zpool add my-raid-z2 log /home/wspeirs/disk5
```

As with a normal vdev, it is possible to mirror a SLOG/SIL vdev. Usually there are better uses for fast storage than mirroring a SLOG/SIL because ZFS design gracefully handles a failed SLOG/SIL. Instead, stripe together multiple, fast disks to provide an even faster SLOG/SIL, as shown:

```
# zpool add my-raid-z2 log /home/wspeirs/disk5 /home/wspeirs/disk6

# zpool status
POOL: my-raid_Z2
STATE: ONLINE
SCAN: none requested
CONFIG:

NAME                         STATE    READ  WRITE  CKSUM
MY-raid_Z2                   Online   0     0      0
    raidz2-0                 Online   0     0      0
        /home/wspeirs/disk1  Online   0     0      0
        /home/wspeirs/disk2  Online   0     0      0
        /home/wspeirs/disk3  Online   0     0      0
        /home/wspeirs/disk4  Online   0     0      0
    logs                     Online   0     0      0
        /home/wspeirs/disk5  Online   0     0      0
        /home/wspeirs/disk6  Online   0     0      0

errors: no known data errors
```

WORKING WITH VDEVS

To extend the capacity of the ARC and, therefore, increase the performance of a zpool, add a second level to the ARC that leverages a faster device. Creating an L2ARC is similar to creating a SLOG/SIL for a zpool except with the cache type instead of the `log` type, as shown here:

```
# zpool add my-raid-z2 cache /home/wspeirs/disk5
cannot add to 'my-raid-z2': cache device must be a disk or disk slice
```

Using files instead of actual disks, the `zpool` command complains about not using a real disk. Obviously, this error does not manifest itself in real situations when using an SSD.

CHAPTER 7

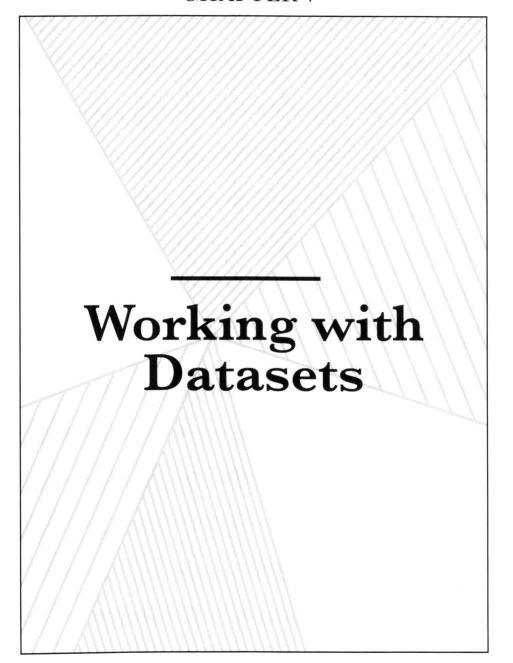

Working with Datasets

WORKING WITH DATASETS

Before beginning to explore the ZFS filesystem, a zpool is needed in which to create the filesystem or dataset. Using the `zpool` command from the previous chapter, a zpool with the label of blackhole that is composed of three top-level vdevs, each consisting of mirroring two disk files, can be created as shown in this example:

```
# zpool status
POOL: blackhole
STATE: ONLINE
SCAN: none requested
CONFIG:

NAME                       STATE   READ  WRITE  CKSUM
blackhole                  Online  0     0      0
  mirror-0                 Online  0     0      0
    /home/wspeirs/disk1    Online  0     0      0
    /home/wspeirs/disk2    Online  0     0      0
  mirror-1                 Online  0     0      0
    /home/wspeirs/disk3    Online  0     0      0
    /home/wspeirs/disk4    Online  0     0      0
  mirror-2                 Online  0     0      0
    /home/wspeirs/disk5    Online  0     0      0
    /home/wspeirs/disk6    Online  0     0      0

errors: no known data errors
```

Referring to the `zpool list`, these three top-level vdevs create a pool of 240MB:

```
# zpool list
NAME       SIZE  ALLOC  FREE  EXPANDSZ  FRAG  CAP  DEDUP  HEALTH  ALTROOT
blackhole  240M  70K    240M  -         1%    0%   1.00X  ONLINE
```

The `zpool` command creates, modifies, and destroys zpools, and their associated vdevs. The `zfs` command creates, modifies, and destroys datasets. There are five types of datasets in ZFS: filesystem, volume, snapshot, clone, and bookmark. People often interchange the term dataset with filesystem in discussion of ZFS, as a filesystem is the most common and default type of dataset. Technically, dataset is an umbrella term that includes all five types.

ZFS COMMANDS

Just like the `zpool` utility, the `zfs` utility has commands. Find a detailed description of each command in the `zfs` utility man page. Below is a list of each command with a brief description:

Table 6: ZFS commands

Command	Description
CREATE	Creates new ZFS filesystem or volume.
DESTROY	Destroys specified dataset.
SNAPSHOT | SNAP	Creates snapshot with given name.
ROLLBACK	Reverts dataset to specified snapshot.
CLONE	Creates clone of given snapshot.
PROMOTE	Promotes clone to filesystem so it is no longer dependent upon its "origin" snapshot.
RENAME	Renames given dataset.
BOOKMARK	Creates bookmark of given snapshot.
LIST	Lists property information for given dataset.
GET	Displays properties for specified dataset.
SET	Sets property to given value for specified dataset.
INHERIT	Clears specified property causing it to be inherited from its ancestor.
UPGRADE	Displays list of files systems that are not using most recent version.
USERSPACE	Displays space consumed by, and quotas on, each user in specified filesystem or snapshot.
GROUPSPACE	Displays space consumed by, and quotas on, each group in specified filesystem or snapshot.
MOUNT	Displays mounted filesystems or mounts specified filesystem.
UNMOUNT	Unmounts specified filesystem.
SHARE	Shares specified filesystem.

WORKING WITH DATASETS

Table 6: ZFS commands

UNSHARE	Unshares specified filesystem.
SEND	Writes stream representation of specified filesystem, snapshot, or bookmark to standard output.
RECEIVE	Creates filesystem, snapshot, or volume whose contents are read from standard input.
ALLOW	Delegates administrative permissions for specified filesystem or volume to non-privileged user.
UNALLOW	Removes permissions granted with allow command.
HOLD	Adds single reference to specified snapshot.
HOLDS	Lists all existing user references for specified snapshot.
RELEASE	Removes single reference from specified snapshot.
DIFF	Displays difference between two snapshots of specified filesystem.

Just like the `zpool` utility, all `zfs` commands must be run as root.

MANAGING FILESYSTEMS

Filesystems are created using the create command and deleted using the destroy command; akin to the `zpool` command. The similarity in the `zfs` and `zpool` commands makes it easy to manage both datasets and zpools.

Before manually creating a filesystem, note that as soon as a zpool is created, a filesystem is implicitly created and mounted in Linux. Looking at the output from the `df` command below, there is a ZFS filesystem mounted at `/blackhole`:

```
# df -T
NAME          TYPE    1K-BLOCKS   USED        AVAILABLE   USE%   MOUNTED ON
/dev/sda1     ext4    20509308    11788740    7655712     61%    /
blackhole     zfs     212864      0           212864      1%     /blackhole
```

Change directories into this implicit filesystem at `/blackhole` and use some of the space by creating a file, as shown here:

```
/blackhole# echo "hello world" > hello
```

As expected, this space shows up as used in the `df` listing:

```
# df -T
NAME         TYPE   1K-BLOCKS  USED      AVAILABLE  USE%  MOUNTED ON
/dev/sda1    ext4   20509308   11788828  7655624    61%   /
blackhole    zfs    212736     128       212736     0%    /blackhole
```

Use the create command to create a filesystem in our blackhole zpool:

```
# zfs create blackhole/test1
```

Datasets in ZFS form a hierarchy via their mount points much like the ext2/3/4 filesystems in Linux. For example, it's common in Linux to have a root filesystem (/) and a boot filesystem (/boot) possibly with different characteristics. When looking at the output from `df` it is clear that /boot is mounted under /, or is a child of /. However, unlike normal Linux filesystems, ZFS's parent-child relationship means that properties set in the parent level, are inherited by the child.

It is not advised to use the `df` command to list the mounted ZFS datasets. Here is the `df` command output after creating the test1 dataset in the blackhole zpool.

```
# df -h
NAME              SIZE  USED  AVAIL  USE%  MOUNTED ON
blackhole         208M  0     208M   0     /blackhole
blackhole/test1   208M  0     208M   0     /blackhole/test1
```

 Use caution here. Don't assume that this output provides two files systems (blackhole and blackhole/test1) that each contain 208MB of space. Always relying on the `zfs` command, as output from `df` is deceptive. Learn how to read the `zfs list` output properly to avoid confusion:

WORKING WITH DATASETS

```
# zfs list
NAME              USED    AVAIL    REFER    MOUNTEDPOINT
blackhole         251K    208M     19K      /blackhole
blackhole/test1   19K     208M     19K      /blackhole/test1
```

Because datasets in ZFS form a hierarchy, the space used also works the same way. For example, creating a 1MB file in the blackhole/test1 filesystem, and zfs list appears to show that both blackhole and blackhole/test1 datasets use 1MB of space:

```
# zfs list
NAME              USED    AVAIL    REFER    MOUNTEDPOINT
blackhole         1.09M   207M     19K      /blackhole
blackhole/test1   1.02M   207M     1.02K    /blackhole/test1
```

Remember the rule that the parent inherits all used space of its children. The **REFER** column shows how much space is referenced by that dataset. Take care here as well. Simply adding up space quantities in the **REFER** column is incorrect. Don't forget about space used by snapshots and clones that refer to the same data. The dataset of a snapshot is not copied but simply referenced. This enables users to store 2GB of data in a 1GB zpool.

Creating another filesystem under test1 and another filesystem under blackhole shows more clearly how ZFS uses space:

```
# zfs list
NAME                    USED    AVAIL    REFER    MOUNTEDPOINT
blackhole               1.13M   207M     19K      /blackhole
blackhole/test1         1.04M   207M     1.02K    /blackhole/test1
blackhole/test1/test2   19K     207M     19K      /blackhole/test1/test2
blackhole/test2         1.04    207M     1.02M    /blackhole/test2
```

Both blackhole/test1/test2 and blackhole/test2 do not have associated files, and so do not use any space. This is indicated by both the USED and REFER columns.

Use the `zfs destroy` command to remove the filesystems created:

```
# zfs destroy blackhole/test2
# zfs list
NAME                    USED    AVAIL   REFER   MOUNTEDPOINT
blackhole               1.26M   207M    19K     /blackhole
blackhole/test1         1.04M   207M    1.02M   /blackhole/test1
blackhole/test1/test2   19K     207M    19K     /blackhole/test1/test2
```

If we attempt to destroy the blackhole/test1 dataset, ZFS helpfully tells us that we cannot do so because it has children. Though we can recursively destroy the datasets using the `-r` flag, as shown here:

```
# zfs destroy blackhole/test1
cannot destroy 'blackhole/test1': filesystem has children
use '-r' to destroy the following datasets:
blackhole/test1/test2

# zfs destroy -r blackhole/test1
# zfs list
NAME            USED    AVAIL   REFER   MOUNTEDPOINT
blackhole       76K     208M    19K     /blackhole
```

MANAGING SNAPSHOTS

One of the attractive features of ZFS is the ability to snapshot a filesystem at a given point in time, without the need to copy the entire contents of the filesystem. For example, we can re-create the test1 filesystem under blackhole, add a file "hello" with the contents

WORKING WITH DATASETS

"hello world," and then take a snapshot of the filesystem giving it the name snapshot1. Creating this snapshot is shown here:

```
# zfs snapshot blackhole/test1@snapshot1
# zfs list -t snapshot,filesystem
NAME                USED    AVAIL   REFER   MOUNTEDPOINT
blackhole           108K    208M    19K     /blackhole
blackhole/test1     29K     208M    20K     /blackhole/test1
blackhole           9K      -       19.5K   -
```

Note that the snapshot does not use any space as it simply points to all data in blackhole/test1. If we copy hello into a new file called world, and relist, the snapshot now uses a small amount of space, as shown here:

```
# zfs list -t snapshot,filesystem
NAME                USED    AVAIL   REFER   MOUNTEDPOINT
blackhole           102K    208M    19K     /blackhole
blackhole/test1     29K     208M    20K     /blackhole/test1
blackhole           9K      -       19.5K   -
```

This is because the snapshot tracks changes made between itself and the actual filesystem. Snapshots can be accessed in two ways: mounting the snapshot and via the invisible (not hidden) `.zfs` directory.

Mounting a snapshot works in the same way as mounting any other filesystem in Linux, but explicitly pass the type, `zfs`:

```
# mount -t zfs blackhole/test1@snapshot1 /mnt
# df -h
FILESYSTEM                  SIZE    USED    AVAILABLE   USE%    MOUNTED ON
/dev/sda1                   20G     12G     7.3G        61%     /
blackhole                   208M    0       208M        0%      /blackhole
blackhole/test1             208M    0       208M        0%      /blackhole/test1
blackhole/test1@snapshot1   208M    0       208M        0%      /mnt
```

Listing the contents of `/mnt` shows the snapshot contents of blackhole/test1. Snapshots are read-only and unmodifiable because a snapshot is only a point-in-time capture of another dataset. For a modifiable version of a snapshot, create a clone.

It is also possible to access snapshots via the invisible `.zfs` directory found at the root of each filesystems. Note, this directory is not hidden, but invisible:

```
/blackhole/test1# ls -la
total 3
drwxr-xr-x 2 root root   4 Nov 19 14:33 .
drwxr-xr-x 3 root root   3 Nov 19 14:18 ..
-rw-r--r-- 1 root root  12 Nov 19 14:19 hello
-rw-r--r-- 1 root root  12 Nov 19 14:33 world

/blackhole/test1# cd .zfs

/blackhole/test1/.zfs# ls
shares   snapshot
```

Access the invisible directory by changing your current directory. Inside the `.zfs` directory are two directories: `snapshot` and `shares`. The snapshot directory has one directory for each snapshot taken for that filesystem. Browse this snapshot by simply accessing the directory, as shown here:

```
/blackhole/test1/.zfs/snapshot/snapshot1# ls -l
total 1
-rw-r--r-- 1 root root 12 Nov 19 14:19 hello
```

To make accessing this directory more user-friendly, set the `snapdir` property to `visible` to render the `.zfs` directory visible, as shown here:

```
# zfs set snapdir=visible blackhole\
```

Use the `zfs destroy` command to remove snapshots as with any other dataset, as shown here:

```
# zfs destroy blackhole/test1@snapshot1
# zfs list -t snapshot,filesystem
```

WORKING WITH DATASETS

MANAGING CLONES

NAME	USED	AVAIL	REFER	MOUNTEDPOINT
blackhole	102K	208M	19K	/blackhole
blackhole/test1	29K	208M	20K	/blackhole/test1

Clones are simply modifiable snapshots. Think of them as a filesystem that lives in a parallel universe to an existing filesystem. The advantage of a clone over simply copying the contents of a filesystem, is that a clone only uses the space needed to track the changes to the original filesystem. Much like a snapshot, all existing data is represented by a pointer back to the original data.

To create a clone, first create a snapshot of the filesystem. Then, create a clone using the desired snapshot and indicate the desired location as shown here:

```
# zfs clone blackhole/test1@snapshot1 blackhole/clone1
# zfs list -t all
```

Notice that clone1 uses much less space than test1; the space that is

NAME	USED	AVAIL	REFER	MOUNTEDPOINT
blackhole	428K	208M	19K	/blackhole
blackhole/clone1	1K	208M	20K	/blackhole/clone1
blackhole/test1	20K	208M	20K	/blackhole/clone1
blackhole/test1@snapshot1	0	-	20K	-

used is for simple bookkeeping by ZFS. Observe changes made to clone1 in the example shown:

```
# dd if=/dev/urandom of=data bs=1024 count=1024
# zfs list -t all
```

NAME	USED	AVAIL	REFER	MOUNTEDPOINT
blackhole	1.13M	207M	19K	/blackhole
blackhole/clone1	1.01M	207M	1.02K	/blackhole/clone1
blackhole/test1	20K	207M	20K	/blackhole/clone1
blackhole/test1@snapshot1	0	-	20K	-

Use the `zfs destroy` command to destroy clones as with any other dataset in ZFS, as shown here:

```
# zfs destroy blackhole/clone1
```

MANAGING ZFS VOLUMES

ZFS can expose a zpool as a block device. This feature creates a ZFS volume (zvol). A zvol exposes all features of a zpool (RAID-Z, snapshots, replication, etc.) in the form of a block device, enabling other filesystems that do not natively have these features to inherit them. For example, a zvol can be created and initialize as an ext4 filesystem. Now the ext4 filesystem can be snapshotted and replicated to another machine. Creating a zvol is similar to creating a ZFS filesystem, as shown here:

```
# zfs create -V 10m blackhole/myvol
```

The -v flag, followed by a size, indicates creation of a zvol of the given size. Take note that the zvol instantly consumes space:

```
# zfs list
```

NAME	USED	AVAIL	REFER	MOUNTEDPOINT
blackhole	10.7M	197M	19K	/blackhole
blackhole/clone1	10.6M	208M	8K	-

The zvol uses consumes space in the zpool because the pool could run out of space (as it is shared amongst all the datasets) and prevent the zvol

WORKING WITH DATASETS

from providing all the space that was allocated. There is no magic here, the space is allocated using a refreservation, which is shown here:

```
# zfs get refreservation blackhole/myvol
```

NAME	PROPERTY	VALUE	SOURCE
blackhole/myvol	refreservation	10.6M	local

To save on space, a sparse volume can be created using the `-s` flag, as shown here:

```
# zfs create -V 10m -s blackhole/sparsevol
# zfs list
```

NAME	USED	AVAIL	REFER	MOUNTEDPOINT
blackhole	11.0M	197M	19K	/blackhole
blackhole/clone1	10.6M	208M	8K	-
blackhole/test1	8K	197M	8K	-

```
# zfs get refreservation blackhole/myvol blackhole/sparsevol
```

NAME	PROPERTY	VALUE	SOURCE
blackhole/myvol	refreservation	10.6M	local
blackhole/sparsevol	refreservation	none	default

Take great care when using a sparse zvol. As much as possible, keep the promises made to the consumer to provide a certain amount of space for the block device.

A newly created zvol is exposed to the system as any other block device in /dev. Create an ext4 filesystem on the myvol zvol in the usual manner, as shown here:

```
# mkfs.ext4 /dev/zvol/blackhole/myvol
mke2fs 1.42.13 (17-May-2015)
Discarding device blocks: done
Creating filesystem with 10240 1k blocks and 2560 inodes
Filesystem UUID: e500c543-6cf1-4924-b303-f7a6c7cec127
Superblock backups stored on blocks:
8193
```

```
Allocating group tables: done
Writing inode tables: done
Creating journal (1024 blocks): done
Writing superblocks and filesystem accounting information: done
```

This ext4 filesystem is now mounted and used like any other ext4 filesystem, but it is backed by a set of devices in a configuration equivalent to RAID-10 and supports all the advanced features of a zpool.

QUOTAS AND RESERVATIONS

Quotas are a common concept in filesystems. Quotas prevent a runaway process or user from filling up the shared resource, the disks. Reservations, on the other hand, are a concept that is distinct to ZFS. Because every dataset that belongs to a zpool shares the capacity of the zpool, reserve a certain amount of space for a dataset so it is not starved by other datasets in the same zpool. Both quotas and reservations are set using ZFS properties:

- **quota** – maximum amount of space dataset and its children can use
- **refquota** – maximum amount of space dataset can use, excluding children
- **reservation** – minimum capacity available to dataset and its children
- **refreservation** – minimum capacity available to dataset, excluding children

Setting a quote or reservation is as simple as setting the property on the dataset. For example, to ensure that the `blackhole` dataset, and all its children, never use more than 10MB of space, set the quota property for that dataset in this manner:

```
# zfs set quota=10M blackhole
# zfs get quota,refquota,reservation,refreservation blackhole
```

WORKING WITH DATASETS

NAME	PROPERTY	VALUE	SOURCE
blackhole	quota	10M	local
blackhole	refquota	none	default
blackhole	reservation	none	default
blackhole	refreservation	none	default

```
# zfs list
```

NAME	USED	AVAIL	REFER	MOUNTEDPOINT
blackhole	111K	9.89M	19K	/blackhole
blackhole/test1	20K	9.89M	20K	/blackhole/test1

An attempt to write more data to the filesystem than the quota results in an error as expected:

```
# dd if=/dev/zero of=./data bs=1024 count=2000000
dd: error writing './data': Disk quota exceeded
10114+0 records in
10113+0 records out
10355712 bytes (10 MB, 9.9 MiB) copied, 3.0518 s, 3.4 MB/s
```

Resetting or updating a quota or reservation is as simple as updating the property for the dataset. To remove the quota on blackhole simply set the property to none:

```
# zfs set quota=none blackhole
# zfs list
```

NAME	USED	AVAIL	REFER	MOUNTEDPOINT
blackhole	414K	208M	19K	/blackhole
blackhole/test1	20K	208M	20K	/blackhole/test1

CHAPTER 8

Advanced Filesystem Features

ADVANCED FILESYSTEM FEATURES

ZFS has several advanced filesystem features. Modern filesystems use features such as compression, deduplication, and encryption. However, other capabilities, such as bookmarks and delegation are distinct to ZFS.

The common, filesystem features -- compression, deduplication, and encryption -- are all controlled by ZFS properties on the dataset. When enabling or disabling these properties, the feature is not retroactive. For example, enabling compression does not instantly (or even start a background process to) compress already written data. Any new data written after the property is enabled will be compressed. The easiest way to take a filesystem without a feature enabled and enable it across all data, is to send it to another dataset with the feature enabled. More about sending datasets in ZFS Send and Receive section.

COMPRESSION

Compression is the ability to remove redundancy in files to allow the writing of more data to a zpool than the capacity of the zpool. Compression on a per-file level is used all the time. Adding compression to a filesystem provides data saving benefits without having to change any of your programs. Compression can also actually speed up reading data from disk. This is because less data must be read from the disk, but it comes at the cost of CPU overhead. This is the standard space-time tradeoff found in many places in computer science.

Enable compression using the compression property on a dataset. ZFS has four compression algorithms: LZ4, LZJB, GZIP, and ZLE. Examining the differences between the compression algorithms is beyond the scope of this book. However, when in doubt, use the LZ4 algorithm. Also, note the results of simply setting `compression=on` defaults to the LZJB algorithm being used as shown here:

```
# zfs set compression=lz4 blackhole
# zfs get compression blackhole
NAME                     PROPERTY           VALUE        SOURCE
blackhole                compression        lz4          local
```

With compression enabled, write some random data to the filesystem and see how well LZ4 does, as shown here:

```
# dd if=/dev/urandom of=/blackhole/random.dat bs=1024 count=10240
10240+0 records in
10240+0 records out
10485760 bytes (10 MB, 10 MiB) copied, 0.751892 s, 13.9 MB/s
```

Let's check how well the compression algorithm does in compressing data by looking at the compressratio property in this example:

```
# zfs get compressratio blackhole
NAME                     PROPERTY           VALUE        SOURCE
blackhole                compressratio      1.00x        -
```

Because we wrote random data, there is no compression; the ratio is 1. If writing highly compressible data (e.g., the text of this book) to the filesystem this ratio changes:

```
# zfs get compressratio
NAME                     PROPERTY           VALUE        SOURCE
blackhole                compressratio      1.05x        -
```

As more data is compressed, the value of the ratio goes up. On average, and with lots of data, LZ4 produces a compression ratio around 2.1. To understand how much space the filesystem uses, look at the used and logicalused properties shown here:

```
# zfs get used,logicalused blackhole
NAME                     PROPERTY           VALUE        SOURCE
blackhole                used               10.2M        -
blackhole                logicalused        10.7M        -
```

ADVANCED FILESYSTEM FEATURES

The used property shows how much space is consumed by the data; whereas, the logicalused property shows how much data is stored if it were uncompressed.

To disable compression, simply set the property to `off`:

```
# zfs set compression=off blackhole
```

As stated above, this change does not affect data already written to the filesystem.

DEDUPLICATION

Deduplication is similar to compression, but works on larger chunks of data. Whereas compression looks for repeated patterns and removes them, deduplication looks for entire, repeated blocks and removes them. Deduplication is a great method for handling large chunks of data that are exactly the same in your filesystem.

Every write to disk must consult the deduplication table which is cached in memory. 1TB of deduplicated data uses 2.5GB to 5GB of memory. ZFS limits the amount of memory used for deduplication to 25% of the system's memory (configurable as shown in Chapter 9, Performance Tuning). This has the potential to rob the system of a lot of memory. The table is also persisted to disk as it is needed between reboots. Reading the entire deduplication table into memory is required, when the `zfs_dedup_prefetch property` is enabled, every time a deduplicated zpool is mounted. This can cause long pauses during mounting, and requires lots of disk I/O. Enabling deduplication also increases the amount of time it takes to free a block. Therefore, destroying filesystems and snapshots takes longer than without deduplication enabled. To see if deduplication is right for a particular dataset, consult Chapter 9, Performance Tuning, and run the `zdb` utility with the `-s` flag. This simulates deduplication on your dataset and advises on the potential gains.

With these considerations in mind, if deduplication still makes sense for your dataset, enabling it is as easy as setting the deduplication property on the dataset, as shown here:

```
# zfs set dedup=on blackhole/deduped
```

Much like compression, deduplication only affects newly written data. Therefore, optimally, enable deduplication when creating a dataset. Disabling deduplication is as simple as unsetting the property, as shown below:

```
# zfs set dedup=off blackhole/deduped
```

Again, this change to the property only affects newly written data.

ENCRYPTION

Encrypted ZFS filesystems work almost identically to unencrypted ZFS. The difference is that encryption keys are required to provide read and write access to the filesystem. To create an encrypted filesystem, three properties are set: `encryption`, `keyformat`, and `keylocation`. Unlike compression and deduplication, encryption must be set at dataset creation, and cannot be changed. This means that all data in an encrypted dataset will be secured using the same underlying encryption algorithms.

The `encryption` property specifies which algorithm to use to encrypt the filesystem. The default value is off which means that encryption is disabled for the filesystem. Currently, all options use AES as the block cipher in either CCM or GCM modes and with key lengths of 128,

ADVANCED FILESYSTEM FEATURES

192, and 256 bits. The encryption property is set to one of the following values: `on | off | aes-128-ccm aes-192-ccm, aes-256-ccm aes-128-gcm, aes-192-gcm, aes-256-gcm. Setting the value to on uses the default cipher suite, aes-256-ccm`, which may change in future versions. Unlike `compression=on` however, once an encryption suite is chosen for a given filesystem it will not dynamically change in future versions.

The `keylocation` and `keyformat` properties configures how the key is loaded when the filesystem needs to be decrypted. `keyformat, keylocation`. The `keyformat` property determines how the key is formatted. Table 7 specifies the options for the `keyformat` segment of the `keysource` property.

Table 7: *keyformat options.*

KEYFORMAT	DESCRIPTION
raw	The bytes of the key are provided
hex	Each byte of the key is provided as a 2-byte hexadecimal code.
passphrase	The key is an 8 to 64 ASCII character passphrase.

When using a `raw` or `hex` format, the key is always 256 bits (or 32 bytes) long, regardless of the encryption suite. The hex representation is 64 characters in length.

⚠ **Always** generate keys via a secure random number generator.

The `passphrase` format relies on a cryptographic algorithm, PBKDF2, to convert an arbitrary length passphrase into a cryptographic key. Tune the algorithm to balance security and performance. The optional `pbkdf2iters` property specifies how many iterations the algorithm uses to convert a passphrase into a cryptographic key. Increasing this number increases the amount of computation required to mount the filesystem, but can increase security. The increased computational cost is only incurred during mounting, and does not affect read or write performance.

The `keylocation` property specifies where the key is located. There are only two options: `prompt` and a file URI. Specifying `prompt` allows the user to specify the key at the terminal. The key may also be passed in via standard input for easier automation. However, care must be taken using this method as it could expose the key in the Linux process tree. The other option is a file URI of format `file://absolute_path_to_file`. This allows the optional storage of the key on a removable USB drive or other device.

```
# zfs create -o encryption=on -o keyformat=passphrase \
  -o keylocation=prompt blackhole/crypt
Enter passphrase:
Re-enter passphrase:

# zfs get encryption,keyformat,keylocation blackhole/crypt
NAME                PROPERTY        VALUE           SOURCE
blackhole/crypt     encryption      aes-256-ccm     -
blackhole/crypt     keyformat       passphrase      local
blackhole/crypt     keylocation     prompt          local
```

By default, a child of an encrypted filesystem inherits the encryption algorithm and key of the parent filesystem. In other words, the key is implicitly loaded for this filesystem when the parent's key is loaded. A different key for the child filesystem can always be specified by providing a new `keyformat` and `keylocation` manually during filesystem creation. It is not possible to create an unencrypted child filesystem of an encrypted parent. However, the encryption algorithm for the child may be different than that of the parent.

At creation of a filesystem, the keys are optionally loaded and unloaded via `zfs load-key` and `zfs unload-key` respectively. Check the status of any filesystem keys via the keystatus property as shown here:

ADVANCED FILESYSTEM FEATURES

```
# zfs umount blackhole/crypt
# zfs unload-key blackhole/crypt
# zfs get keystatus blackhole/crypt
```

NAME	PROPERTY	VALUE	SOURCE
blackhole/crypt	keystatus	unavailable	-

```
# zfs mount blackhole/crypt
cannot mount '/blackhole/crypt': encryption key not loaded
# zfs load-key blackhole/crypt
Enter passphrase for 'blackhole/crypt':
# zfs mount blackhole/crypt
# zfs get keystatus blackhole/crypt-
```

NAME	PROPERTY	VALUE	SOURCE
blackhole/crypt	keystatus	available	-

For convenience, the `zpool import` and `zfs mount` commands also have a `-l` flag that will attempt to load the keys of every filesystem that requires them.

The `zfs` change-key command changes the key encrypting a dataset without having to re-encrypt the entire dataset. This requires that the old key is already loaded. Alternatively, the `-l` flag can be used to load the key before changing it. With no options specified, the `keylocation` and `keysource` properties remains the same, and only the key used to decrypt the filesystem changes. Alternatively, specify new values for the `keylocation`, `keyformat`, and `pbkdf2iters` properties to modify the way in which the key is loaded. :

```
# zfs change-key -o keyformat=hex blackhole/crypt \
  -o keylocation=file:///home/blackhole/blackhole.key
# zfs get encryption,keyformat,keylocation blackhole/crypt
```

NAME	PROPERTY	VALUE	SOURCE
blackhole/crypt	encryption	aes-256-ccm	-
blackhole/crypt	keyformat	hex	local
blackhole/crypt	keylocation	file:///home/blackhole/blackhole.key	local

Optionally, use `zfs change-key` with a new `keysource`, `keylocation` and `keyformat` to break the default key inheritance from a parent filesystem. This is useful when deciding that a child filesystem is to have a key different than its parent. The dataset may be re-linked later with zfs change-key -i.

SCRUB AND RESILVER

As mentioned previously, everything in ZFS is checksummed. These checksums ensure that the correct data is always returned to the reading process properly, or an error is thrown. ZFS always provides correct data and does this on-the-fly. ZFS verifies checksums and uses redundant copies (from RAIDZ, mirrors, or if the copies property is set to > 1) to repair any bad blocks while reading from the device. This on-the-fly repairing of data can lull administrators into a false sense of security. If data is written to disk but never read, its integrity is never checked. This is where scrubbing and resilvering come into play.

Scrubbing a zpool forces ZFS to walk over every block in the zpool and verify its checksum. Unlike the traditional `fsck` utility, a scrub occurs while the zpool is online and in use. To initiate a scrub use the zpool utility and the scrub command, as shown here:

```
# zpool scrub blackhole
```

The scrub process runs in the background, so the utility does not return any output. Monitor the status of the scrub using the status command shown here:

```
# zpool status
POOL: blackhole
STATE: ONLINE
SCAN: scrub repaired 0 in 0h0m with 0 errors on Thu Dec 29 17:48:03 2016
CONFIG:
```

ADVANCED FILESYSTEM FEATURES

```
NAME                         STATE    READ  WRITE  CKSUM
blackhole                    Online   0     0      0
  mirror-0                   Online   0     0      0
    /home/wspeirs/disk1      Online   0     0      0
    /home/wspeirs/disk2      Online   0     0      0
  mirror-1                   Online   0     0      0
    /home/wspeirs/disk3      Online   0     0      0
    /home/wspeirs/disk4      Online   0     0      0
  mirror-2                   Online   0     0      0
    /home/wspeirs/disk5      Online   0     0      0
    /home/wspeirs/disk6      Online   0     0      0
errors: no known data errors
```

The `errors:` line at the bottom of the status command, notes any data errors. These errors are fixed automatically if replication (`mirror`, RAIDZ, or `copies`) is configured. Cancel a scrub using the `-s` flag as shown here:

```
# zpool scrub -s blackhole
```

A resilver is like a scrub, except a resilver only examines the data that ZFS knows to be out-of-date. A scrub will inspect all the data. A resilver occurs when a device is brought back online on a mirror or RAIDZ vdev in a zpool. There is no zpool command to initiate a resilver, as it occurs automatically. Both scrubbing and resilvering are very I/O intensive operations and impact system performance while occurring. Chapter 9, Performance Tuning, explains how to configure the system to modify performance tradeoffs.

ZFS SEND AND RECEIVE

The send and receive commands of the `zfs` utility are used to send filesystem data to standard out and receive filesystem data from standard in. Because all data is sent to standard out and read from standard in, all Linux command line redirection tools can be used. Because an entire filesystem is sent/received, snapshots ensure the version of the filesystem being sent is does not change during the process of sending. Consider using unmounted filesystems and read-only zpools as an option. To send a snapshot of a filesystem, simply use the send command of the `zfs` utility and the name of the snapshot as noted in this example:

```
# zfs send blackhole/original@sn1 > /tmp/sn1
```

The sn1 snapshot of the blackhole dataset is now saved in the file `/tmp/sn1`. For ease of use, copy this snapshot to a USB stick and insert into a new system. Let's view some information about the sent snapshot using the `zstreamdump` utility in this example:

```
# zstreamdump < /tmp/sn1
BEGIN record
  hdrtype = 1
  features = 4
  magic = 2f5bacbac
  creation_time = 58659d75
  type = 2
  flags = 0x0
  toguid = 527a4b128d51a6b4
  fromguid = 0
  toname = blackhole/original@sn1
END checksum = 14d5188d2fc40a/aa8b2f5e1ab2f6df/8265bcb1b84d4982/be2e45f1794d5ea7

SUMMARY:
Total DRR_BEGIN records = 1
Total DRR_END records = 1
Total DRR_OBJECT records = 10
Total DRR_FREEOBJECTS records = 0
Total DRR_WRITE records = 94
Total DRR_WRITE_BYREF records = 0
Total DRR_WRITE_EMBEDDED records = 0
Total DRR_FREE records = 0
```

ADVANCED FILESYSTEM FEATURES

```
Total DRR_SPILL records = 0
Total records = 106
Total write size = 11195904 (0xaad600)
Total stream length = 11229816 (0xab5a78)
```

Recreate the snapshot on a new (or the same) system using the receive command of the zfs utility as shown here:

```
# cat /tmp/sn1 | zfs receive blackhole/copy
```

In this case, the filesystem is replicated on the same system. The `zfs receive` command creates a new filesystem, blackhole/copy, and copies all data there. The `zfs list` command shown here verifies this:

```
# zfs list
NAME                USED    AVAIL   REFER   MOUNTEDPOINT
blackhole           30.4M   178M    10.1M   /blackhole
blackhole/copy      10.0M   178M    10.0M   /blackhole/copy
blackhole/original  10.0M   178M    10.0M   /blackhole/orginial
```

The true power of the `zfs send/receive` commands is apparent when data is sent from one machine to another. Because data is written to standard out and read from standard in, the `ssh` utility to securely transfer a snapshot of a filesystem from one machine to another.

Because snapshots are sent, it is possible to indicate to the `zfs send` command that only the difference between two snapshots must be sent, and not the entire filesystem. In this example, writing another 1MB of data to blackhole/original, then taking another snapshot, it can be indicated that only the new 1MB must be sent, instead of the total 11MB filesystem:

```
# zfs snapshot blackhole/original@sn2
# zfs send -i blackhole/original@sn1 blackhole/original@sn2 > \
  /tmp/sn2
# ls -lh /tmp/sn1 /tmp/sn2
-rw-r--r-- 1 root root  11M /tmp/sn1
-rw-r--r-- 1 root root 1.1M /tmp/sn2
```

This is a great way to incrementally backup a filesystem to another machine. The system only sends the changes between snapshots, reducing network and processing overhead. The receive side of the command does not change for incremental backups, as shown in this example:

```
# cat /tmp/sn2 | zfs receive blackhole/copy
```

 Take caution when using incrementals for backups to remote machines. If the remote filesystem changes in any way, then an incremental is unable to be applied to the remote filesystem.

Two common ways to prevent modification of the filesystem are to set the `readonly` property on the filesystem, or to unmount the filesystem after receiving the incremental backup. Setting the `readonly` property is a great way to prevent changes as the filesystem can still receive incremental snapshots, but none of the files inside the filesystem can be changed. If changes do occur, the `-F` flag on the receiving side can force a backup to a common snapshot. Avoid using the `-F` flag and attempting to find a common snapshot (a dangerous game); it is best to simply prevent changes.

Note that when using the `-i` flag to send incremental snapshots, the two sides must be in sync with respect to snapshots, or snapshots will be lost. For example, if blackhole/original has @sn1, @sn2, and @sn3, but blackhole/copy is missing @sn2, an attempt to issue the following command will result in @sn2 not being created:

```
# zfs send -i blackhole/original@sn1 blackhole/original@sn3 \
| zfs receive blackhole/copy
```

This is because blackhole/copy is missing the intermediate @sn2. The `zfs send` command has a `-I` flag to remedy this problem. The `-I` flag creates any intermediary snapshots that are missing from the receiving side. However, because the `zfs send` command is unidirectional, all data associated with @sn2 and @sn3 are sent. So, while the `-I` flag is more robust than the `-i`

ADVANCED FILESYSTEM FEATURES

flag, it comes at the cost of sending possibly redundant snapshots. The `zfs send/receive` commands have numerous other command line options that print statistics, provide more verbose output, enable deduplication (which can consume a lot of memory, so use carefully), enable resumable sends, and even provide a dry-run option. More detailed information about `zfs send/receive` can be found in the man page for the `zfs` utility.

BOOKMARKS

Snapshots must be used to send and receive filesystem changes. The problem with using snapshots is that snapshots can accumulate if numerous changes are made to the filesystem. To reduce the amount of space used in the zpool by snapshots, create a bookmark for the oldest snapshot. Bookmarks are light versions of snapshots. Bookmarks do not track changes to blocks, only to the youngest birthtime of a block in a snapshot. When a `zfs send` command is issued, all blocks in the snapshot with birthtimes younger than the one in the bookmark are sent. This allows for incrementals to be sent, saving bandwidth, and also allows all of the changes a snapshot would typically track to be discarded. Bookmarks are much like snapshots, except they use a # symbol in their name instead of an @ symbol as shown in this example:

```
# zfs bookmark blackhole/original@sn2 blackhole/original#bm2
# zfs list -t all
```

NAME	USED	AVAIL	REFER	MOUNTEDPOINT
blackhole	32.8M	175M	10.1M	/blackhole
blackhole/copy	11.0M	175M	11.0M	/blackhole/copy
blackhole/copy@sn1	9K	-	10.0M	-
blackhole/copy@sn2	0	-	11.0M	-
blackhole/original	11.0M	175M	11.0M	/blackhole/original
blackhole/original@sn1	9k	-	10.0M	-
blackhole/original@sn2	0	-	11.0M	-
blackhole/original#bm2	-	-	-	-

The bookmark #bm2 now contains the birthtime of the youngest block in the @sn2 snapshot. When sending an incremental, this bookmark is used in place of the snapshot as shown here:

```
# zfs send -i blackhole/original#bm2 blackhole/original@sn3
```

CHAPTER 9

Performance Tuning

PERFORMANCE TUNING

ZFS can be tuned at two levels: the system as a whole, and per-dataset/per-zpool. The parameters that control the entire ZFS are found in /sys/module/zfs/parameters on Linux. There are 128 parameters that change the way ZFS operates. Most of these settings are found in the zfs-module-parameters man page. When changing one of these parameters, the effect is immediate, but does not persist across reboots. To keep a setting across a reboot, add it to the proper config file for the ZFS module. The way in which this is done can vary between Linux distributions.

Per-dataset/per-zpool parameters are properties set on individual datasets or zpools. The list of available properties for datasets and zpools is in Chapter 4, Filesystem. Not all properties take effect immediately, and some must be set during dataset or zpool creation.

COLLECTING STATS

Before tuning a system for performance, statistics must be collected to identify the bottleneck. Besides the normal Linux tools (htop, iotop, etc.), there are two ZFS-specific utilities to help identify bottlenecks: zpool iostat and zdb. The zpool utility has an iostat command that provides information about the I/O statistics of pools on the system. When the command is run without parameters, it provides the total or average stats from the start of the machine (or creation of the pool) as in this example:

```
# zpool iostat
                CAPACITY        OPERATIONS      THROUGHPUT
POOL         ALLOC     FREE    READ    WRITE   READ    WRITE
------       -----    -----    ----    -----   ----    -----
blackhole    10.3M    230M     0       0       3       18
```

Provide a number after the command, and it runs continuously providing point-in-time snapshots of the statistics of the pools that many seconds apart. The first line is the total or average since the start of the machine, with the point-in-time measurements following. Using Ctrl-C stops the command as shown here:

```
# zpool iostat 1
               CAPACITY         OPERATIONS      THROUGHPUT
POOL        ALLOC    FREE     READ    WRITE    READ    WRITE
------      ----     ----     ---     ----     ----    ----
blackhole   10.3M    230M     0       0        3       18
blackhole   10.3M    230M     0       0        3       0
blackhole   10.3M    230M     0       0        3       0
blackhole   10.3M    230M     0       0        3       0
^C
```

Use the **-v** flag to obtain a breakdown of statistics for individual vdevs that compose a zpool, as shown in this example:

```
# zpool iostat -v
                         CAPACITY         OPERATIONS      THROUGHPUT
POOL                  ALLOC    FREE     READ    WRITE    READ    WRITE
------                ----     ----     ---     ----     ----    ----
blackhole             10.3M    230M     0       0        3       18
  mirror              3.34M    76.7M    0       0        0       6
    /home/wspeirs/disk1  -       -      0       0        69      50
    /home/wspeirs/disk2  -       -      0       0        47      50
  mirror              3.11M    76.9     0       0        1       5
    /home/wspeirs/disk3  -       -      0       0        48      50
    /home/wspeirs/disk4  -       -      0       0        49      50
  mirror              3.81M    76.2     0       0        1       6
    /home/wspeirs/disk5  -       -      0       0        48      50
    /home/wseirs/disk6   -       -      0       0        48      50
-----------                    ----    ----    ----     ----    ----
```

PERFORMANCE TUNING

Note that ZFS's per-device numbers are not accurate as raw values. These numbers are however, proportionally accurate. This is because the ZFS module does not lock certain kernel structures while performing the measurements, so values are constantly changing during the measurement reading.

Another tool for digging deep into ZFS benchmarking is `zdb`. The `zdb` utility, or ZFS debugger, reads information about a ZFS pool from disk. The `zdb` utility is fragile and opaque as stated in the man page for the utility:

> It is a not a general purpose tool and options (and facilities) may change.
> The output of this command in general reflects the on-disk structure of a ZFS pool, and is inherently unstable. The precise output of most invocations is not documented, a knowledge of ZFS internals is assumed.

There are a few useful features of the utility that provide insight into the performance of a zpool. The `-c` flag verifies the checksums and print statistics about the blocks used in the system, as shown here:

```
# zdb -c blackhole
Traversing all blocks to verify metadata checksums and verify
nothing leaked ...
loading space map for vdev 2 of 3, metaslab 4 of 5 ...
  No leaks (block sum matches space maps exactly)

    bp count:              169
    ganged count:            0
    bp logical:       11843584    avg:  70080
    bp physical:      10643968    avg:  62982    compression:   1.11
    bp allocated:     10760704    avg:  63672    compression:   1.10
    bp deduped:              0    ref>1:     0   deduplication: 1.00
    SPA allocated:    10760704    used:  4.28%

    additional, non-pointer bps of type 0: 24
```

The `-s` flag displays statistics on I/O operations for the pool, as shown here:

```
# zdb -s blackhole
```

	CAPACITY		OPERATIONS		BANDWIDTH		ERRORS		
DESCRIPTION	USED	AVAIL	READ	WRITE	READ	WRITE	READ	WRITE	CKSUM
blackhole	10.3M	230M	52	0	50.5K	0	0	0	0
mirror	3.34M	76.7M	16	0	15.5K	0	0	0	0
/home/wspeirs/disk1	-	-	395	0	1.41M	0	0	0	0

	CAPACITY		OPERATIONS		BANDWIDTH		ERRORS		
DESCRIPTION	USED	AVAIL	READ	WRITE	READ	WRITE	READ	WRITE	CKSUM
/home/wspeirs/disk2	-	-	383	0	994K	0	0	0	0
mirror	3.11M	76.9M	14	0	14.0K	0	0	0	0
/home/wspeirs/disk3	-	-	370	0	996K	0	0	0	0
/home/wspeirs/disk4	-	-	304	0	995K	0	0	0	0
mirror	3.81M	76.2M	22	0	21.0K	0	0	0	0
/home/wspeirs/disk5	-	-	351	0	1001K	0	0	0	0
/home/wspeirs/disk6	-	-	361	0	1000K	0	0	0	0

The -s flag (notice the capital) simulates deduplication on the zpool and print statistics. This is a useful tool to observe the impact of enabling deduplication on a zpool. The command will show the savings and overhead of deduplication as shown here:

```
# zdb -S blackhole
Simulated DDT histogram:

BUCKET              ALLOCATED                       REFERENCED
REFCNT      BLOCKS  LSIZE   PZISE   DSIZE   BLOCKS  LSIZE   PSIZE   DSIZE
-------------
1           86      10.6M   10.1M   10.1M   86      10.6M   10.1M   10.1M
TOTAL       86      10.6M   10.1M   10.1M   86      10.6M   10.1    10.1M

dedup = 1.00, compress = 1.06, copies = 1.00, dedup * compress \
copies = 1.06
```

While outside the scope of performance tuning, the zdb utility also aid in extreme circumstances to recover a zpool by forcing the use of older transactions with the -F flag. **Only use when all other avenues for repair have been exhausted.**

PREFETCHING

Both Linux and ZFS have the concept of prefetching information from disk into a cache for improved performance. It is assumed that if some part of a file is accessed, that the rest of that file will be accessed soon. The bottleneck in accessing data from spinning drives is lining up the

PERFORMANCE TUNING

heads to read the data. If this is achievable ahead-of-time, the overall system can feel much more responsible.

ZFS supports two types of prefetching: vdev and file. Vdev prefetching works by reading a few additional blocks off a vdev than requested in the hopes of retrieving useful metadata. If the metadata is found, it is inserted into a standard in-memory LRU cache, not the ARC. If a process then requests this metadata, it is fetched from the in-memory cache instead of the disk. The size of the cache is set to the number of devices that compose the vdev, times the value in the `zfs_vdev_cache_size` parameter. Most installations set this value to zero, disabling the cache. That is because only on systems where complicated metadata manipulation occurs often (including complex or large directory structures), is enabling vdev prefetching useful.

The `zfs_vdev_cache_max` and `zfs_vdev_cache_bshift` parameters also control how the vdev prefetch works. The `zfs_vdev_cache_max` parameter specifies the minimum amount of data read from a vdev for prefetch to occur. If a read request is made to the vdev that is less than `zfs_vdev_cache_max`, more data than the request is read. The additional amount read is computed by bit shifting a single bit by the amount in the `zfs_vdev_cache_bshift` parameter. Using the default values of 16K (16384) and 16 for the `zfs_vdev_cache_max` and `zfs_vdev_cache_bshift` parameters respectively, a read of 8K results in an actual read of 64K. Whereas, a read of 32K does not activate the prefetch and results in a read of exactly 32K.

File prefetching simply reads more of the file than asked, with the expectation that this data will be requested later. ZFS prefetches data when there is 4GB of memory present on the system, and disables it when there is less. Change this behavior by setting the `zfs_prefetch_disable` parameter. Setting this parameter to `1` disables this auto-tuning, and always enables prefetching.

TRANSACTION GROUP TUNING

A transaction group is the set of changed blocks or new blocks written between checkpoints. Transaction groups improve the efficiency of ZFS by allowing multiple modifications to a single block to be grouped together and performed in memory before being flushed to disk. The amount of time between checkpoints has a dramatic effect on the overall performance of ZFS. If checkpoints occur too often, multiple changes to the same block are all persisted to disk, slowing the system down. If checkpoints occur too infrequently, the sheer number of changes persisted cause momentary pauses to the system.

There are two parameters that determine when a checkpoint occurs: `zfs_txg_timeout` and `zfs_dirty_data_max`. The `zfs_txg_timeout` parameter is the value a timer is set to, in seconds, that triggers a checkpoint if nothing else has triggered a checkpoint. The default value is 5s. This is reasonable on most systems. The `zfs_dirty_data_max` parameter is the maximum amount of data, in bytes, a pending transaction group can have before being flushed to disk. If a transaction group reaches this size, it is flushed to disk regardless of how much time is left on the transaction group timer. The default of this value is set to 10% of the available memory.

Tuning these parameters comes down to two factors: the amount of memory on the system, and the throughput the devices in the zpool can provide. In most modern systems, the amount of memory far outweighs the throughput of the devices in the zpool. It is not uncommon to have 32GB or 64GB of RAM on a system with only two spinning disks in a mirrored zpool. Writing 3.2GB, or 10% of 32GB, to disk can take 10s of seconds. This means that

PERFORMANCE TUNING

while ZFS is trying to write data to disk, the next transaction group timer is expiring causing even more writes. This can lead to a system that appears to lock up because of disk I/O. Decreasing the `zfs_dirty_data_max` parameter can help on systems with a lot of memory, but very small device throughput. On systems where this is opposite, say a laptop with only 4GB of memory but very fast SSDs, the value could be increased or the `zfs_txg_timeout` parameter shortened so writes occur more frequently. These frequent writes finish quickly because of the high throughput of SSDs.

Beyond these two parameters, and when a transaction group is flushed to disk, ZFS has a complex system for throttling writes and delaying transaction groups. Throttling occurs when a program is streaming writes to ZFS faster than the disk can persist them. ZFS accommodates this by artificially adding a delay to the `write` command before returning. This slows the process streaming the writes to a speed equal to the throughput of the device. The man page for `zfs-module-parameters` has an entire section on ZFS Transaction Delay.

SCRUBS AND RESILVERS

ZFS has five I/O classes it uses to manage I/O: `sync_read`, `sync_write`, `async_read`, `async_write`, and `scrub/resilver`. I/O operations are prioritized in that order. Each I/O class is controlled by a pair of parameters: `zfs_vdev_sync/async_read/write_min/max_active` and `zfs_vdev_scrub_min/max_active`. These parameters control the minimum and maximum I/Os active to each device. There is also an aggregate maximum for all classes, as shown here: `zfs_vdev_max_active`.

Adjusting these parameters is a tradeoff between throughput and latency. Most devices increase throughput as the number of concurrent operations increases, but latency suffers. There is also a point at which adding more operations will not increase throughput and may even cause a degradation in performance. How the I/O scheduler uses these parameters to schedule I/O is best described by the ZFS I/O Scheduler section of the `zfs-module-parameters` man page:

> The scheduler selects the next operation to issue by first looking for an I/O class whose minimum has not been satisfied. Once all are satisfied and the aggregate maximum has not been hit, the scheduler looks for classes whose maximum has not been satisfied. Iteration through the I/O classes is done in the order specified above. No further operations are issued if the aggregate maximum number of concurrent operations has been hit or if there are no operations queued for an I/O class that has not hit its maximum. Every time an I/O is queued or an operation completes, the I/O scheduler looks for new operations to issue.

In most situations, changing these parameter defaults causes more harm than good. A lot of investigation and metrics gathering is needed to know when and by how much to change any parameters. This is especially difficult because of the precise timing needs of metrics gathering (usually when the system is under normal and peak load). Testing on production machines is usually not a viable option.

That said, tuning the scrub/resilver parameters can greatly impact your system. Because scrubs and resilvers do not occur during normal operation, changing parameters that dictate the minimum and maximum outstanding I/O operations for these classes can have predictable results. Increasing both `zfs_vdev_scrub_min_active` and `zfs_vdev_scrub_max_active` multiplies the number of concurrent I/O operations dedicated to a scrub/resilver, decreasing the amount of time a scrub/resilver takes. If such maintenance only occurs during off-hours or during a maintenance window, then increasing these values benefits the overall system with little disadvantage. There is a price to increasing these values, read and write operations can be queued behind scrub/resilver operations.

PERFORMANCE TUNING

Scrubs and resilvers have two other parameters the I/O scheduler uses to decrease their priority to prevent these operations from negatively impacting system performance: `zfs_scrub_delay` and `zfs_resilver_delay`. These parameters denote the number of ticks to delay prior to issuing an I/O operation when a read or write I/O operation has occurred within the past `zfs_scan_idle ticks`. The idea is to only issue scrub/resilver I/O operations when the system is idle. To determine when the system is idle, `ZFS waits zfs_scrub/resilver_delay` X `zfs_scan_idle` ticks for no other I/O operations to occur, then starts a scrub or resilver I/O operation. To effectively decrease the amount of time a scrub or resilver takes, set both parameters to zero. Doing so means that ZFS does not wait for the system to be idle before issuing a scrub or resilver I/O operation.

 Changing these parameters along with the `zfs_vdev_scrub_min_active` and `zfs_vdev_scrub_max_active` parameters can cause the system to essentially refuse reads and writes in favor of scrub and resilver operations. **Change these parameters with caution.**

VOLBLOCKSIZE AND RECORDSIZE

There are two properties, `volblocksize` and `recordsize`, that can dramatically affect the performance, both in size and throughput, of ZFS. The `volblocksize` property specifies the block size of a ZFS volume. It is important to match the `volblocksize` of the ZFS volume to the block size of the filesystem residing on that volume.

The `recordsize` property is a bit more complicated and setting it to the wrong value can cause internal fragmentation, wasting space on the system and degrading throughput. RAIDZ always allocates blocks in multiples of the parity level, plus one. For example, RAIDZ-1 allocates two blocks at a time, RAIDZ-2 three blocks at a time, and RAIDZ-3 four blocks at a time. This can cause some weird interactions as shown in Table 8. In each instance, a single, 8KB block is being written. The columns show the layout for devices with sector sizes of 512B and 4KB. The numbers are the amount of data + parity + padding required. The last column shows the percent of wasted space (parity + padding) for the two devices.

Table 8: *Various zpool configurations and the space wasted.*

CONFIGURATION	512B SECTORS	4KB SECTORS	% WASTED
Mirroring	16 + 0 + 0 = 16	2 + 0 + 0 = 2	0%
RAIDZ-1	16 + 1 + 1 = 18	2 + 1 + 1 = 4	11% & 50%
RAIDZ-2	16 + 2 + 0 = 18	2 + 2 + 2 = 6	11% & 66%
RAIDZ-3	16 + 3 + 1 = 20	2 + 3 + 3 = 8	20% & 75%

Mixing the wrong combination of sector sizes and RAIDZ configurations can leave your disks wasting as much as 75% of their capacity.

DATABASES

ZFS has many attractive features for use with databases. You can snapshot a database to provide a read-only copy for development, or clone the entire dataset for a staging or testing environment. Tuning the `recordsize` property to match the expected record size of the database prevents write amplification and makes ZFS extremely performant. Write amplification occurs when a small change requires a lot of data to be written to disk. For example, if the `recordsize` property is set to 128KB and the database wants to update an 8KB record in the middle of that block, ZFS must read 128KB from disk, modify the 8KB in the middle, and then write the entire 128KB back to a new location on-disk (because ZFS is a copy-on-write filesystem).

PERFORMANCE TUNING

To get the most performance out of ZFS, always match the database record size to the ZFS `recordsize` property. For example, InnoDB and XtraDB by Percona both use 16KB block sizes, while the MySQL MyISAM engine and PostgreSQL use 8KB block sizes. It is best to create a separate dataset for your database and tune its `recordsize` property appropriately.

Another slightly, counter-intuitive performance improvement that can be made for databases is enabling compression. By enabling compression, ZFS can read more data off the disk faster. Most systems have far more CPU resources to decrypt data than disk throughput. The lz4 compression algorithm has a built-in, early abort feature which disables compression if it does not provide any benefit.

Adjusting the replication of metadata is also a potentially huge performance gain for databases. With small record sizes, the metadata to data ratio is much higher than when using 128KB record sizes. To compensate for this, ZFS added the `redundant_metadata` property. Setting this property to `most` reduces the number of copies of some metadata improving performance.

Caching offers another area of opportunity for performance improvement for databases. Most database engines have some level of caching to improve performance. ZFS also caches data, which results in a wasteful double-cache. To prevent this, set the `primarycache` and `secondarycache` properties to `metadata` rather than the default of all. This tells ZFS to only cache metadata, leaving data caching to the database engine.

Index

A

ARC 4, 9, 21, 37-39, 40, 62, 64, 100

Async 102

B

Blackhole 66-78, 81-83, 85-93, 96-99

Block size 10, 104

C

Cache 9, 20, 21, 35, 37-40, 64, 99, 100, 106

Checkpoint 34-36, 101

Checkpoints 4, 34

Checksum 27, 42, 50, 57, 87, 89

Clone 31, 67, 73, 74, 105

Clones 10, 25, 31, 34, 42, 70, 75

Compression 43, 45, 52, 80-84, 98, 106

Copy-on-write 9, 10, 14, 17, 20, 31, 105

Create 10, 20, 21, 35, 54-56, 58, 61, 62, 66-69, 71, 73-76, 83, 85, 92, 106

D

Database 10, 11, 35, 36, 105, 106

Dataset 24, 26, 41-45, 48, 66, 67, 69-71, 73, 75, 77, 78, 80, 82, 83, 86, 87, 89, 96, 105, 106

Datasets 8, 41, 42, 51, 52, 66-72, 74-78, 80, 96

Deduplication 5, 82

Destroy 43, 54, 68, 71, 73, 75

Device 14, 16, 17, 24, 35, 54-56, 62-64, 75, 76, 85, 87, 88, 98, 102

Df 68, 69, 72

Disk 9, 10, 14, 15, 20, 26, 29, 30, 34-38, 48, 5-52, 55, 61-64, 66, 80, 82, 87, 98-106

E

Encryption 3-5, 8, 47-50, 83

Ext2/3/4 9, 10, 27, 69

F

File 3, 9, 10, 14, 20, 26, 28-31, 35, 36, 51, 56, 68, 70-72, 80, 85, 86, 89, 96, 99, 100

Filesystem 5, 8, 9, 20, 21, 33, 45, 72, 76, 79, 96

I

Intent log 20

K

Kernel 9, 30, 39, 55, 98

L

L2ARC 4, 19, 21, 37, 38, 39, 62, 64

Label 14, 54, 61, 66

Linux 8-10, 14, 15, 27, 30, 37, 39, 40, 50, 51, 68, 69, 72, 85, 89, 96, 99

List 14, 26, 29, 36, 39, 40, 41, 54-57, 61, 66, 67, 69-76, 78, 90, 92, 96

Logical vdev 16

Logical vdevs 15

M

Memory 9, 20, 21, 37, 40, 48, 82, 92, 100-102

Metadata 11, 29, 30, 44, 50, 51, 98, 100, 106

Mirror 14-16, 18, 55-61, 63, 66, 88, 97-99

Mirror-0 57-61, 66, 88

Mirrored 14-16, 18, 55-61, 63, 66, 88, 97-99

Mount 26, 67, 69, 72, 84, 86

P

Parameters 96, 100-104

Performance 8, 11, 16, 18, 20, 21, 35, 38, 39, 40, 51, 62-64, 84, 88, 96, 98, 99, 101, 103, 104, 106

Physical vdev 14, 16, 29, 54

Properties 4, 41, 45

R

RAID-Z 4, 5, 15-18, 61, 62, 75

RAID-Z1 15, 61, 62

RAID-Z2 17, 19, 61, 62

RAID-Z3 17, 19, 61

Readonly 42, 44, 91

Receive 44, 45, 68, 88, 90, 91, 92

Record size 10, 11, 105, 106

Redundancy 15-18, 59, 61, 62, 80

Reference 26, 27, 34, 36, 68

Resilver 5, 87

S

Scrub 5, 87

Send 5, 80, 88

SLOG 4, 5, 19-21, 62-64

Snapshot 67

Space 10, 18, 25, 31, 50, 51, 56, 61, 67-72, 74-77, 80, 81, 82, 92, 98, 104, 105

T

Throughput 96, 97, 101-104, 106

Transaction group 29, 34, 36, 101, 102

U

Uberblock 20, 25, 29, 34, 36

V

Vdevs 14-16, 18-20, 24, 27, 34, 54-56, 58-62, 64, 66, 67, 97

Volume 15, 24, 27

Z

Zdb 83, 96, 98, 99

ZFS 1, 3-5, 8-11, 14, 15, 17, 19-27, 29-31, 33-38, 40, 41, 45, 47-52, 54, 55, 63, 66-71, 74, 75, 77, 80, 82, 83, 87, 88, 96, 98-106

Zpool 5, 16, 18, 24, 25, 29-31, 36, 41, 42, 45, 50, 51, 54-64, 66-70, 75, 77, 80, 82, 86-88, 92, 96-99, 101, 105

ABOUT THE AUTHOR

William Speirs is the Senior Director of Datto Labs, Datto's Research and Development department, charged with improving resource usage in Datto's data center and developing new product ideas. He has previously worked as a researcher for the government, as an adjunct professor at the University of New Haven, and as a Research Assistant Professor at Purdue University. He holds a PhD in Computer Science from Purdue University, and a BS in Computer Science from Rensselaer Polytechnic Institute.

Made in the USA
Middletown, DE
15 February 2019